BEQUEST & BETRAYAL

Bequest & Betrayal

MEMOIRS OF A
PARENT'S DEATH

Nancy K. Miller

New York   Oxford
Oxford University Press
1996

Oxford University Press

Oxford   New York
Athens   Auckland   Bangkok   Bombay
Calcutta   Cape Town   Dar es Salaam   Delhi
Florence   Hong Kong   Istanbul   Karachi
Kuala Lumpur   Madras   Madrid   Melbourne
Mexico City   Nairobi   Paris   Singapore
Taipei   Tokyo   Toronto

and associated companies in
Berlin   Ibadan

Library of Congress Cataloging-in-Publication Data

Miller, Nancy K., 1941–
Bequest and betrayal : memoirs of a parent's death /
by Nancy K. Miller
p. cm   ISBN 0-19-509130-2
1. Bereavement—Psychological aspects.   2 Parents—Death—
Psychological aspects.   3. Miller, Nancy K., 1941– .   4. Death in
literature.   5. Autobiography—Psychological aspects.   I. Title.
BF575.G7M536   1996
155.9'37—dc20   96–19954
Rev.

1 3 5 7 9 8 6 4 2

Printed in the United States of America
on acid-free paper

Acknowledgments

Whatever I was supposed to be writing in the spring of 1991—OK, a study of French eighteenth-century novels—it was soon displaced by an irresistible need to think about the death of my parents, a subject that demanded exploration. My editor, Liz Maguire, encouraged me and I remain happily indebted to our collaboration—over many, many lunches. I can't imagine having done this book with anyone else. In the process, friends, colleagues, and students read and commented on drafts of chapters and sometimes—endearingly—the whole thing. I am especially grateful to Rachel M. Brownstein, Susan Gubar, Katharine Jensen, Marianne Hirsch, Elizabeth Houlding, Alice Y. Kaplan, Rolf Meyersohn, Sally O'Driscoll, Jane Opper, Michael Rothberg, and Ellen Sweet.

My sister Ronna Texidor, my aunt Fay Horwitz, my cousins Carol Greilsheimer and Alan Miller helped me in ways big and small by telling me their view of our collective family plots; Donald Petrey explained what all this might have to do with DNA. Two friends from Los Angeles, one old and one new, saw me through the penultimate stages of the manuscript. Margaret Waller, queen of manuscript revision, gently and artfully forced me to own up to what I was reluctant to avow. With the uncommon patience and generosity that are his, Daniel Hayes got me to think about the emotional truth of a writer's page and about the reader's need for autobiography's secrets. I have a very special debt to my student Elizabeth Hollow, without whose remarkable editorial savvy and vision this book might never have seen the light of day. I also wish to thank the wonderfully responsive audiences at the college campuses where I was invited to read my work in progress. Last, and of course in crucial ways, first, I want to express my gratitude to Margaret Mandel, with whom I spent zillions of hours trying to figure out what this book was really about and why I had to write it.

My oldest and as always greatest debt, however, is to my dear and irreplaceable friend Carolyn G. Heilbrun, whose enlivening intelligence and inimitable example of wit and perseverance kept me from feeling lonely while writing about being alone.

I want to thank my new editor at Oxford, Susie Chang, for her gracious assistance. And Victoria P. Rosner, for her inspiriting eleventh-hour intervention.

I am deeply grateful to the John Simon Guggenheim Memorial Foundation for providing me with the time to undertake this project.

Some of the chapters in this book have been published in different form as essays. I would like to thank the *Massachusetts Review*, *m/e/a/n/i/n/g*, *differences*, and Routledge for their kind permission to reprint.

An early version of "My Father's Penis" appeared as an afterword to *Refiguring the Father: New Feminist Readings of Patriarchy*, edited by Patricia Yaeger and Beth Kowaleski-Wallace (Southern Illinois University Press, 1989), and as the final chapter of my *Getting Personal: Feminist Occasions and Other Autobiographical Acts* (Routledge, 1991).

The published translations of the French works have occasionally been modified.

Contents

Prologue:
Writing a Parent's Death
xi

1. Family Plots
3

2. Childless Children: Bodies and Betrayal
27

3. Mothers and Daughters: The Price of Separation
61

4. The Arts of Survival: Mom, Murder, Memory
101

5. Outing the Dead
131

6. Unbillable Hours
173

Epilogue:
Postmortem
189

Works Cited
195

For DSP
Who lived through it with me

Prologue:

WRITING A
PARENT'S DEATH

Children begin by loving their parents. As they grow
older they judge them; sometimes they forgive them.
OSCAR WILDE, *The Picture of Dorian Gray*

The origins of this book are inseparable from the loss of my parents.
My mother's death was a shock. An athletic nonsmoker, she was
diagnosed as having lung cancer days after her sixty-eighth birthday
and died a few months later. But it was only in the years following
her death, when my father became physically and mentally crippled
by Parkinson's disease, that I began to think and to write about the
end of life.

Death, literary critics have not failed to point out, is good for
narrative. It gives shape to the messiest of plots and retrospectively
conveys meaning to whatever has come before. In autobiography,
the death of others always provides unexpected narrative benefits. It
tells us something important about who we are, especially when the
death is that of a parent. The loss of a parent and the work of self-
examination—how we watch our parents die; how we live with ourselves, and them, after they are gone—lie at the heart of an aston-
ishing number of contemporary memoirs. I'm writing here about
how I've tried to make sense of my life as a daughter in the wake of
my parents' death, and how reading the memoirs of writers coming
to terms with their loss has helped but also complicated my task. As
a reader of autobiography, I perform an awkward dance of embrace

and rejection: He's just like me, she's not like me at all. As I write myself into and out of other stories, in counterpoint to dramas lived on other stages, scenes from my personal history take on new significance. Can my story—or yours—ever be more than that: a dialogue enacted with other selves?

The death of parents—dreaded or wished for—is a trauma that causes an invisible tear in our self-identity. In the aftermath of a parent's death, which forces the acknowledgment of our shared mortality, loss and mourning take complex paths, since our earliest acts of identity are intimately bound up with our relation to the dead parent. But the closure produced by the end of their plot does not signal the end of ours. With the loss of the second parent, the child/parent dialogue moves into the space of memory and writing. When we become adult orphans of whatever age, our stories continue—sometimes on paper—now authored by us, with others listening. We don't choose our families, but we get to revise their myths.

Why write about the dead? Because the dead are alive in us, and in our face. We are inhabited by their desires, keenly attuned to the demands of what Virginia Woolf calls "invisible presences," the forces that keep the subject of a memoir "tugged this way and that every day of his life." A dead parent, Jacques Derrida observes, "can be more alive for us, more powerful, more scary, than the living." Haunted by our pasts, we are forged in relations of likeness and difference. Showing our faces, telling ourselves, cannot help but betray the others who live on in our heads and dreams. Writing about oneself entails dealing with the ghostly face in the mirror that is and isn't one's own.

Reacting to loss can take the form of a literary obligation: "I thought: my father is gone. If I do not act quickly," Paul Auster reflects in *The Invention of Solitude*, "his entire life will vanish along with him." But there is no single pattern of response among writers who, like Auster, set out to retrieve and restore the life of the missing parent. "I must remember accurately," Philip Roth recalls telling himself in *Patrimony*, "remember everything accurately so that when he is gone I can re-create the father who created me." Writing a parent's death is a way to repair a broken connection. "I imagined," French novelist Annie Ernaux admits in *A Man's Place*, a memoir about her father's life, "that I had nothing else to learn from him. . . . Maybe I am writing because we no longer had anything to say to each other." The reparation of belatedness requires engaging with the dead.

Autobiography is fundamentally a democratic enterprise. As memorialists of the dead, writers join readers who find themselves caught up (as we cannot fail to be) in the situations of loss and grief that come with the territory of human ties. Whatever our singular destinies, such memoirs offer the reader an occasion to reflect autobiographically on the terms of these foundational relations: what it means to lose one's parents, and how to make sense of their absence—and continuing presence. (In a bookstore one day on the Upper West Side of Manhattan, I overheard a man ask the clerk where to find books on death and dying; the clerk directed him to the "recovery" section.)

Like classic autobiographies that chart an individual history from birth to crowning accomplishment, memoirs are documents about building an identity—how we come to be who we are as individuals—and a crucial piece of that development takes place in the family. This is not necessarily the good news. "When Tolstoy wrote that all happy families are alike, what he meant," Susan Cheever observes in *Treetops*, "was that there are no happy families. The family is as confining as it is nurturing." But happy or unhappy, families provide a scenario in which we get to try out and perform ideas about ourselves, who we would like to be—within limits. The limits set by the family constitute the blueprint of a self, the outlines of autobiographical space. We could also think of this as the family plot; especially if we include within this notion of plot a burial plot (the plot that ultimately awaits us all). Writing in the journal *Tikkun*, Art Spiegelman explains that *Maus: A Survivor's Tale*—his two-volume comic book account of his parents' Holocaust experience—supplied a "focus for dealing with the issues that were important to me: my parents, my ethnic background, the ghosts of the dead." Under many guises, the project of autobiographical writing is tied to this intergenerational, historical, and spectral matrix of identifications. We elaborate an individual identity in relation to that set of finalities which are also possibilities, for the present and for the future.

But what happens to our idea of self when there is no generation to follow, when we are childless? What happens to the idea of mourning and legacy when the plot of generations ends with us? I want to insist on the inordinate power of that plot to shape our profoundest ideas of self and other, a power that emerges with peculiar intensity at the moment of a parent's death—for all, but with an edge of violence for those of us without children to follow. We need a language and stories for an exchange between generations that bypasses the body and the family: bonds of paper, not only bonds of blood. We are also connected by books and the friendships that grow out of them.

Unlike the trauma that can radically revise the course of a young person's life, losing a parent in middle age is a drama of a more subtle sort: fully embarked on lives of our own, sometimes with children, we are no longer young, and yet in that primal relation, we are still children. We expect our parents to die, especially when they are old and we are well into middle age. But despite our knowledge, their death comes as a surprise. The manner of death always seems to feel unexpected, a desolating blow. The end of life is not, as Simone de Beauvoir puts it in *A Very Easy Death*, natural: "You die from *something*." The pain of death resides in its details.

"Watching a parent grow is one of the most reassuring experiences anyone can have," Margaret Mead asserts in her autobiography, *Blackberry Winter*. "A privilege," she concludes, "that comes only to those whose parents live beyond their children's early adulthood." The countertruth of contemporary culture in which longevity has outstripped ethics is that watching a parent shrink is one of the most devastating experiences anyone could have. Parents, it seems, live too long or not long enough. "I don't want to be a burden on you girls," my father would say in the early days of his widowerhood, hanging heavily on my sister and me as we staggered with him, shuddering at the irony of his words, but laughing with him all the way down the steep hill to his apartment building on Riverside Drive. Then he was a burden—overwhelmingly—for several years as he first lost control of his body, then his mind. The end of life is not about what you want, certainly not about what you deserve.

Although national differences separate the writers of these memoirs, their books participate in a common project: telling the story of parents and children as adults confronted with the peculiarly modern horror of technologically advanced styles of dying—and living—that often make the experience of losing a parent more unbearable than the loss itself. In the face of postmodern indifference, these writers are passionately committed to the project of personal history.

Memoirs about the loss of parents show how enmeshed in the family plot we have been and the price of our complicity in its stories. The death of parents forces us to rethink our lives, to reread ourselves. We read for what we need to find. Sometimes, we also find what we didn't know we needed.

My paternal grandmother, Sadie S. Kipnis, New York, circa 1910.

1

FAMILY PLOTS

Mourning is immensely reassuring because it convinces
us of something we might otherwise easily doubt: our
attachment to others.

ADAM PHILLIPS, *Terrors and Experts*

*When my mother died, I thought my real life would begin. The war
between us showed no signs of abating, even though we were both weary of
it. "Put your affairs in order," the doctor said, after reading the slides of
her biopsy. The chemotherapy seemed to be having no effect on the progress
of the disease, and after two treatments the oncologist lost interest. She was
sixty-eight and dying of lung cancer. When she realized there was little
hope for recovery, my mother longed for death. But she was too weak and
too confused to do anything about it. Once she seized on the electric toothbrush; brandishing it theatrically, she insisted that she "wanted to put an
end to things." My father removed the toothbrush from the bathroom, even
though the suicide gesture was no more than a charade.*

*My mother felt betrayed by the way age marked her face; no longer
being noticed when she walked into a room pained her. She had lived, she
maintained, the life she had wanted to live. Dying, she wanted to die. She
refused to see any of her friends. "I want to die in the bosom of my family,"
she said, unembarrassed by the lie lurking beneath the cliché. After her
death I was relieved, almost glad that she was gone. I had always thought
that my mother would live into her nineties and that we would go on fighting until I, too, was old—her age. When I scanned her dead body, her face,
looking for signs, I found myself staring into silent hazel eyes. Our last
fight, days before she slipped into a coma, had to do with whether she should*

1

undergo another session of chemotherapy. I couldn't tell if she actually wanted to, or whether in my protest she heard a last chance to do battle. She had taken off her wedding ring with her mother's diamond—the diamond that had spent its first life being pawned every time my grandfather needed cash. She asked my father to put the ring in the vault for safekeeping, like the rest of her "good" jewelry, her specific bequest—for me. But she died wearing earrings—fake pearl studs that had rotted, forgotten for weeks in her pierced ears. The holes were ringed with black. Whenever I fall asleep with my earrings still in my ears, I wake in a small panic, pierced forever with this reminder of her neglect.

Every autobiography requires a coming to terms with the past and a revision of family history. Are these memoirs of a parent's death autobiography? Producing an account of another's life normally belongs to the domain of biography, or the new word in academic circles, *allography*—the biography of another. But when the biographical subject is a member of one's own family, the line between the genres blurs. The term *life-writing* has emerged as a formulation that elides the difference. Life-writing is also the expression Virginia Woolf uses in *Moments of Being* when she evokes the power of her dead mother's voice in her own life, and the role played by the consciousness of others "impinging upon ourselves." I prefer the term *memoir* for literary reasons but for etymological ones as well. By its roots, memoir encompasses both acts of memory and acts of recording—personal reminiscences and documentation. The word *record*, which crops up in almost every dictionary definition of memoir, contains a double meaning too. To record means literally to call to mind, to call up from the heart. At the same time, record means to set down in writing, to make official. What resides in the province of the heart is also what is exhibited in the public space of the world. In this way, memoir is fashionably postmodern, since it hesitates to define the boundaries between private and public, subject and object. "Un-biography," Susan Cheever calls it, "off-center biographies that are as much about me as my subject." These works, critic John Eakin suggests, "offer not only the autobiography of the self but the biography and autobiography of the other." Auto/biographical memoirs are necessarily a hybrid form. "A cross," as Annie

Ernaux describes the project of revisiting her mother's life in *A Woman's Story*, "between family history and sociology, reality and fiction." Whatever the label, the problem remains: whose story is it? Do we even know our own stories? This book reflects the preoccupations of a literary critic who rereads and rewrites herself in the writing of others. In so doing I practice a mode of what Susan Suleiman has recently named "mediated autobiography." I can only, it sometimes seems, read autobiographically.

Philip Roth's *Patrimony* recounts a father's terminal illness and reconstructs his life. Susan Cheever in *Home Before Dark* uncovers fleshy details of John Cheever's intimate sexual life. Simone de Beauvoir's *A Very Easy Death* bears witness to her mother's bodily struggle with cancer. In *Maus*, Art Spiegelman draws the words of his father's Holocaust past. In each case, however differently, a self-portrait of a son or daughter emerges in complex counterpoint to the portrayal of the parent. In these narratives, the parent's death seems to authorize—or at least provide a cover story—for a writer's autobiography. If not explicitly, the memoirs devoted to a dead parent are almost always meditations on a writer's authority, her right to tell this story, the path she followed to telling it. The dead parents' history, especially their family's relation to language and writing, is made to seem inextricable from the story of the living child's vocation.

Colette tells a textbook version of this story in "The Captain," a portrait of her father. Published many years after her parents' deaths in a book of reminiscences entitled *Sido* (her mother's name), this famous vignette evokes the legacy left to the writer by her father, Jules-Joseph Colette. After their father's death, Colette's brother starts sorting the books in the room that served as the paternal library. He calls his sister to show her what he's found on the top shelves. The elaborately handbound volumes called *My Campaigns*, *The Lessons of '70*, *From Village to Parliament*, and so on, but bearing no author's name, turn out to be filled with blank pages, except for the dedication to his beloved wife, Sido: "beautiful, cream-laid paper, or thick 'foolscap,' carefully trimmed, hundreds and hundreds of blank pages. Imaginary works, the mirage of a writer's career." Colette catalogues the family's attempt to use up these pages that never seemed to end, as they tried in vain to cancel out this "proof of incapacity." Describing her own first efforts as a writer, she ponders the effects of this "spiritual legacy" of paternal frustration. "Was that," she wonders, "where I got my extravagant taste for writing on smooth sheets of fine paper, without the least regard for economy?" Covering these pages with her own handwriting, Colette dares to write over "the invisible cursive script" that filled them.

In the early fifties, my father had his Warhol fifteen minutes of fame. He won a suit on behalf of minority stockholders against Howard Hughes and RKO Pictures and made a big splash (he had the check for the lawyers' fees photocopied for posterity). He returned triumphant from California on the first regularly scheduled commercial airline flight nonstop coast-to-coast; a framed certificate that attests to this occasion was signed by the TWA captain; my father's picture and that of his grinning colleagues blown up above it (in the photo they are reading the flight map displayed below), was prominently displayed in the dinette. He had a little brush with B-list celebrity (dinner with sulky-faced Gloria Grahame), met famous men, went to fancy places, and finally made enough money (my mother's dream) for my parents to go to Europe for the first time—deluxe (the Crillon, the Danieli, the Cumberland). The Hughes case was my father's short-lived claim to notoriety. He had the proceedings bound in two leather, gild-trimmed volumes with his name—LOUIS KIPNIS—embossed in gold letters on the spine. The only other spot of glamour in my father's career had come earlier, in the mid-forties when he was retained as Lucille Armstrong's lawyer. How did this happen? The mystery remains but the evidence is there: papers, clippings, photographs signed by Louis Armstrong, whose photographs were mounted on the faux wood-paneled walls in the dinette. My mother (my sister likes to say), a good fifties liberal, would explain, "Oh, we could have had them over, but I wouldn't have felt comfortable." After the Hughes case, my father receded into his normal lawyerly habits, which earned him a living, but nothing more. At the end of his life, he rented space in the glorious Woolworth building, an address his practice never quite lived up to. By then losing ground from Parkinson's, he was mainly handling small estates, writing wills. Sometimes he went to the office just to ride the subway and pick up the mail.

.   .   .

Colette identifies with her father through their shared passion for a writer's tools. But what use does she make of them? I think we can understand the staggering volume of her life's work—once she began she could never stop—as an inverted complicity, writing for her life *against* the secret of his impotence: "My father, a born writer, left few pages behind him." His energy was absorbed by making a fetish of a writer's tools. In this sense, the daughter's writing takes the form of reparation, fulfilling the father's dream in her own life's work. At age fifty, she makes her father's name, the patronymic which is also a woman's name, her signature. Despite the signature, however, the legacy is more parental than simply paternal. Colette's mother, Sido, also wrote. "Sitting at any old table, pushing aside an invading cat, a basket of plums, a pile of linen, or else just putting a dictionary on her lap by way of a desk—Sido really did write. A hundred enchanting letters prove that she did." Colette even flirts with losing in the competition: "Between us two, which is the better writer, she or I? Does it not resound to high heaven that it is she?" But the daughter corrects her mother's letters when she publishes them.

What takes place in the space between a mother and a daughter, a father and a daughter, a daughter who becomes a writer? Between a father and a son who wins a Pulitzer prize for his transfiguration of his father's Holocaust experience? A daughter and a mother, whose writing career was her letters? What's written in a father's invisible cursive script? Invisible, or as in the case of John Cheever, excessively visible typed notebooks? A parent's history is a life narrative against which the memorialist ceaselessly shapes and reshapes the past and tries to live in the present. French philosopher Sarah Kofman takes over possession of her father's fountain pen (her father, a rabbi, dead in Auschwitz), for all her school work. Her many books, she speculates, were "oblique but obligatory crossings to arrive at telling 'that.'" The stakes of telling that story can be high. Kofman killed herself after finally writing *that* book. Life-writing is sometimes fatal.

There seem to be two poles between which memoir writers come to grips with the loss of parents and the pull of their history. These two emotional styles are, broadly speaking, two ways of responding to the death of a loved one that Freud famously called mourning and melancholia. In more popular terms we could think of this process as a movement between acts of forgiveness and resentment. To blame one's parents for one's own misery, as Americans tend to do in this century of therapy culture, is to remain obsessed by one's parents' deficiencies or their failure to love their children, us. The writing of resentment is a mode I admit feeling close to. Resentment is powerful and paralyzing. "Being resentful," as Susan Cheever wittily puts in *A Woman's Life*, "is like taking poison and waiting for the other person to die." This is not a very efficient strategy for dealing with anger and disappointment, especially when the other person is *already dead*.

Forgiveness. We've all been encouraged to grow up and graduate to forgiveness, to accept the limits of our parents' emotional theater. Acceptance, however, can tend toward idealization (just as resentment verges on repudiation), especially when interwoven with compassion in the face of parental vulnerability, as is the case with Philip Roth's hymn to Herman Roth, and Susan Cheever's elegy for John Cheever. Between these poles of resentment and forgiveness (of course, inevitably the two coexist in the same book) are acts of interpretation that I wish to call *realization*. Realization typically begins by unmasking a parent's self-serving construction, taking the edge off one's parent's highly elaborated persona (Vladek Spiegelman's self-righteousness, Françoise de Beauvoir's self-delusion). Realization entails understanding our parents' own unfinished business with their mothers and fathers: seeing it *as theirs*, finding the language in which to name it, and moving on. These acts of revision mean trying to reimagine your parent as a person with whom you can deal. This is the adult version of what in *Bonds of Love* psychoanalyst and feminist theorist Jessica Benjamin calls "mutual recognition," the acknowledgment between child and parent that their related identities are forged in a process of complex negotiation. Forgiveness requires the consciousness of choice: what you choose to identify with, reinventing for yourself—a father's storytelling, a mother's vitality. It means playing your hand and playing to win. This is part of what Freud described—in very different language—as the liberatory work of mourning, as opposed to the unending travail of melancholy in which the mourner fails to separate from the object of loss. Writing a parent's death in literary form displays both the steps toward separation and the tortuous paths of reconnection, after the fact. Grieving and release.

Memoirs that write a parent's death share many generic and thematic features of the elegy. Traditionally, the performance that elegy entails for poets is the act of taking up and revising the precursor's task in their own voices. This is part of the mourning process and requires a break with the past, a separation, and a replacement. Literary critic Jahan Ramazani sees modern elegy as representing what tends to be "unresolved, violent, and ambivalent." Contemporary elegy displays the self-contradictory symptoms of "melancholic" mourning. In these acts of testimony in prose to a past of wounds and pleasures, resentment and forgiveness remain forever entangled.

At the funeral parlor my sister and I were the only ones not obviously saddened by my mother's death. The woman who used to do her hair every week wept openly. Her tennis partners were in shock; she was still winning trophies at the club, playing singles. I went through the service dry-eyed. But at the cemetery, things were different. When it was my turn, according to Jewish custom, to throw a shovelful of dirt onto the coffin, I looked down into the grave and went blank. What was I doing? In that pause the ritual became literalized. My mother was in that box; I was supposed to throw dirt on her. In some archaic zone of my mind in which she remained alive, a revolt took place. I couldn't lift the shovel. I was overtaken by sobs, as though I were betrayed by someone beside herself with grief who lived like a homeless person in the knots of my gut. As I started to collapse onto the ground, one of my cousins led me away from the open grave through the snowy labyrinth of tombstones, over to the car. When we drove back to the city, my father was stonyfaced. He was angry at me, I thought, for making a spectacle of myself. But as usual he said nothing.

We had our last discussion about my mother when the time came to decide what should be written on her gravestone. My sister and I drew the line at having the adjective "BELOVED" inscribed next to the word "MOTHER": she might have been his beloved wife; she wasn't our beloved mother. He said he couldn't understand that. Hadn't she been a good mother, hadn't she done everything for us? Made our clothes, baked cookies, taken us to Girl Scouts? All right, we said, choosing from the limited repertoire of acceptable cemetery language—"DEVOTED." After the unveiling, I took a picture of the tombstone for my father. We all ate lunch in a greasy spoon in Flushing. My father lived another seven years, but his life was over.

The act of leaving home seems particularly fraught for women writers, whose memoirs dwell on the pain of separation from the mother, even when the mother is alive. In her "biomythographical" odyssey *Zami*, poet Audre Lorde invokes the price of separation through a dream she calls "The Last of My Childhood Nightmares." Dated "My Mother's House, July 1954," the dream describes the panic underlying Lorde's need as a young woman to make her own life. Running from a room filled with demons waving their arms wildly, she fears that she "will die of electrocution." She enters her parents' bedroom and picks up a watermelon on a bureau, which then falls crashing to the floor: "The melon splits open, and at the core is a brilliant hunk of turquoise, glowing. I see it as a promise of help coming for me." Suddenly in the dream she understands what has happened: "I realize that in this house of my childhood I am no longer welcome. Everything is hostile to me. This is no longer my home; it is only of a past time." In the dream, this realization is a source of jubilation. She can start her new life. "I am suddenly free to go."

This is no longer my home; it is only of a past time.

Vivian Gornick's *Fierce Attachments* offers one of the most powerful metaphors for the blurring of boundaries between mothers and daughters (in the time of the memoir, the mother is alive). "After Hiroshima," Gornick writes, "dead bodies were found of people who had been wearing printed kimonos when they were killed. The bomb had melted the cloth on their bodies, but the design on the kimonos remained imprinted in the flesh." This style of overidentification between mothers and daughters becomes a form of emotional erasure for the daughter who loses her sense of singularity. "It seemed to me in later years," Gornick concludes, that "the deep nerveless passivity of that time together had become the design burned into my skin while the cloth of my own experience melted away." The task of the memoir is to name the cloth of your own experience.

The Woman Warrior, Maxine Hong Kingston's memoir of growing up Chinese-American in postwar California, shows how separation is often the requirement for a daughter's self-invention. When the girl who becomes a writer (her name, we learn, sounds like "ink") returns as an adult woman to visit her mother Brave Orchid at Turkeyday, she describes her mother's power to enter her mind: "A spider headache spreads out in fine branches over my skull. She is etching spider legs into the icy bone. She pries open my head and my fists and crams into them responsibility for time, responsibility for intervening oceans." Brave Orchid is not happy about the distance that is the condition of their relation, but she yields to its necessity. "Of course, you must go," she reluctantly agrees, naming the daughter with the endearment that speaks their connection: "Good Night, Little Dog."

The death of parents sometimes reveals the cost of shared horizons, of letting our parents live in our heads. In "An Angel at My Table," the second volume of her extraordinary autobiography of vocation, Janet Frame remembers telling a friend (the mentor who has been helping her become a writer by giving her a place to live away from home) the news of her mother's death: "'So what?' he said, showing his bitterness toward his own family. 'Parents are better dead.' Bravely I agreed with him." Frame then goes on to reflect upon her mother's life and what the structure of her parents' relation had meant to her: "My life had been spent watching, listening to my parents, trying to decipher their code, always searching for clues. They were the two trees between us and the wind, sea, snow; but that was in childhood. I felt that their death might expose us," Frame writes, "but it would also let the light in from all directions, and we would know the reality instead of the rumour of wind, sea, snow, and be able to perceive all moments of being." We would go out and weather the storm, unafraid.

My mother and I would be standing face-to-face in the kitchen. This was her territory even though she refused to be defined by it. We would be

*nearing the end of another battle of the wills, woman to girl in the para-
doxes of fifties femininity, hating conformity but sticking to the rules.
Defeated, I would grudgingly perform the demanded hug of capitulation,
keeping a distance hollowed out between our bodies at the center. Marking
her victory, a triumph she had to know was as empty as my embrace, she
would say in a tone that was half menace, half joke: "You'll see when you
have children." It was clear that this expression satisfied something deep
in her. It would often engender the two or three commonplaces that seemed
to make up her own mother's legacy. "Grandma used to say, Little children, little problems; big children, big problems. Grandma used to say, If
I'm not a good mother, who is a good mother?" I could never figure out
what to say in return, especially since I could tell I was getting a mixed
message not only about Grandma, but about her and me. I knew she
didn't think her mother—an uneducated immigrant who had four children (born within the first seven years of her marriage), an endless stream
of demanding relatives, and her own domineering mother to care for—a
model of nurturance. She had no time, my mother said, for any of the
children individually. It was clear that my mother, herself resolutely modern (we had chicken marengo, not chicken soup), felt she had received little
from her mother. Who, then, was the better mother? When I, too, became
a mother with thankless children, would I finally understand that my
mother was a good mother?*

*I realize now that I was meant to find comfort in the inevitability of the
reproductive chain that would ultimately make me both more humble and
more forgiving: I would see. But the chain is broken.*

Critic Henry Louis Gates Jr., frames *Colored People* by a letter to his
daughters, explaining that he knows that the world of his past "has
mysteriously disappeared," and that he wants to record it for them.
He writes in particular about driving along the highway between
small southern towns and getting furious at his older daughter,
Maggie, for the skeptical tone in which she refers to his dead
mother. If "Maggie could have seen Mama," he thinks to himself,
"when she was young and Mama and I would go to a funeral and
she'd stand up to read the dead person's eulogy." If only his daughter could see his mother the way he saw her—at her best, through
his love. *Colored People* is about making sense of generations in a

specific historical moment and finding the story to connect them, after a mother's, a grandmother's death.

The view of the self seen through the logic of generations takes for granted this projection into a future in which we find out who we are in time, through children. "A relation to self," writes cultural critic Michael Warner, that finds "its proper temporality and fulfillment in generational transmission." But what does it mean to think about the death of one's parents when there is no generation to follow? What happens to our legacy if there is no next of kin? These are questions that sometimes arise for the first time at the moment of death, when being the end of the line becomes a literal dead end. When a parent dies, you think about the generations. This one has gone, but through the narrative of replacement, the acts of the next generation try to convert the loss into gain. If you are the child— grown-up and childless yourself in middle age, as I am—the sense of what happens next is less self-evident.

Who will witness your death? Visit your grave? Tell your story?

At the burial service of a friend's father in a pastoral cemetery on Long Island's South Shore, the little grandchildren of a distinguished painter frolicked among the graves set into the hill, oblivious to the gravity of the moment. "I'm so glad the children could be there," my friend said. "It made everything less sad."

Recording the events of everyday life in public spaces, novelist Annie Ernaux reports a conversation overheard at a bus stop. An irritated mother criticizes her adolescent daughter. "I won't always be there! You're going to have to manage all by yourself in life." Ernaux reflects upon the threat. "I can still hear my father or mother saying: 'We won't always be there!' Their intonation. I see the severe expression on their face again. . . . It was a threat from living people; now they're both dead. 'You'll see when we're not there anymore!' The sentence alone remains, absurd, atrocious, when said by others." What do our parents prevent us from seeing? I hear the threat echoing in my head. You'll see. But what will I see when they are no longer there to be my parents? Will I see what it means to be them? What it means to be a parent? If you don't have the experience; if unlike your own parents you don't become parent to a child, is there something crucial you will never see?

When in my prolonged adolescent misery, I agonized over lost chances, my mother would hunt around for some appropriately maternal advice on the subject. To convince me there was still time for happiness, my mother would invoke her mother. "Grandma used to say: You're young as long as you have your parents." As long as my mother was there to repeat that to me, it meant little. After all, I had my parents and they would live forever. Today, friends my age—in our fifties—whose parents are still alive don't seem as close to old age and death as I do. They still complain about their parents ("My mother is driving me crazy") or worry about their health. They still expect something to come from their relationship. Now that both my parents are dead, I begin to take my mother's point.

Why write about the dead? To figure out if they were right.

Philip Roth outlines the emotional context in which he found himself moved to write *The Facts: A Novelist's Autobiography* (published a few years before *Patrimony*): a "crack-up" followed by a "need for self-investigation" and "demythologizing." Roth describes a certain "exhaustion with masks, disguises, distortions, and lies," but he also underscores the effect of his mother's death—"subterraneanly my mother's death is very strong in all this." He wonders whether he isn't writing "as a palliative for the loss of a mother, who still in my mind, seems to have died inexplicably." A dead mother, but also his proximity to his father's anticipated death: "an eighty-six-year-old father viewing the end of life as a thing near to his face as the mirror he shaves in (except that this mirror is there day and night, directly in front of him all the time)." Watching your father watching himself in death's mirror, watching yourself in the same mirror. From this perspective of "parental longing," writing *The Facts* becomes a strategy against loss, a return in writing to a time before the idea of his parents' death (not to say his own) begins to shape the imagination's horizon: how I lived before I realized I was mortal.

Parental longing.

Something crucial is ruptured in our idea of self when a parent dies, even when the consolation of generations exists. This change in itself often becomes the subject of memorialization. In a radio interview after the publication of her prizewinning book, *A Man's*

Place, Annie Ernaux explained that she began dealing with her father's death by writing a novel about him, but then stopped because she felt that to transform his life—his trajectory out of factory work to ownership of a café-grocery—into fiction was a betrayal of his experience. The decision to find a new form (neither biography nor novel) and a style to restore that past life in language ("flat writing") becomes an act of solidarity with the figures of the past that she has left behind, shadows of her previous self.

Leaving home and changing class is one way of feeling that one has betrayed one's parents. But the anxiety over betrayal is palpably at work in these memoirs even if one hasn't gone beyond one's parents in class terms. Often the feeling of betrayal is tied up with the act of disclosure itself, especially when parental values include silence over family matters. In the introduction to *Fathers: Reflections by Daughters*, a collection of autobiographical essays by British women, Ursula Owen remarks that several of the writers said that "the moment their pen touched the paper they felt they were betraying their history; one said that her mother, brothers and sisters seemed to appear as shadows over her shoulder, restraining her." Without betrayal, memoirs would not exist. "It comes to me that in order to write this," Adrienne Rich explains in "Split at the Root," an essay about coming to terms with her Jewish legacy, "I have to be willing to do two things: I have to claim my father . . . and in order to claim him I have in a sense to expose him." Simone de Beauvoir betrays the rules of the class she was born into by becoming an intellectual woman and a free thinker who not only goes public with her sex life (bad enough) but then imagines her parents' unhappy sexual history. Susan Cheever coolly outs John Cheever by publishing excerpts from his diary, thus editing the darkest part of his secret life against the backdrop of his glittery fictions of heterosexual privilege. Invariably, children's right to produce these representations of their parents raises an ethical problem. The dead instantly lose their entitlement to privacy.

On this subject, Spiegelman, like Roth, flaunts the artist's power to override paternal authority. When asked to tell about "Mom," about how he and Anja met, Vladek reminisces about his old girlfriends.

When he then objects that these episodes shouldn't be part of the book because they have nothing to do with the Holocaust, the son counters with his artistic sense of narrative truth: It will be good for the book, make "everything more real, more human." Unconvinced by Art's desire for authenticity, Vladek insists that he leave out these tales of his career as a ladies' man and a heel. "I can tell you *other* stories, but such *private* things, I don't want you should mention." Like Philip, Art promises not to tell. But the biographical memoir is a form of witness that assumes an addressee. Accordingly, Art gets to retell his father's tales his way, draw his lines in the sand. His testimony, too, will be heard by others, even if the original, authorizing version is already on tape—recorded for posterity. The memoir expresses a form of power over its subjects. Like elegy, memoir always gets the last word. Except, perhaps, for the reader.

An urgency creates these memoirs, sometimes completed within the months following a parent's death, sometimes reworked for years, but always under its sign: a narrative of mourning that gives grief a story, loss a semblance of closure. "I wanted my parents' lives to have meant something," Ian Frazier writes in *Family*. "I didn't care if the meanings were far-flung or vague or even trivial.... I hoped maybe I could find a meaning that would defeat death." We comb through our parents' objects, papers, looking for hidden meanings, struck when we are lucky by what Frazier calls "the silent force of a clue." It's not always clear what we are looking for and what finding it would mean.

In *Camera Lucida*, Roland Barthes's famous essay about photography, the critic recounts the experience of searching through his mother's affairs shortly after her death. He was looking, he says, for a photograph that would allow him to write a little volume about his mother, first for himself, then printed for an audience, to ensure that "her memory will last at least the time of my own notoriety." Poring over the pictures, holding them up to the lamp, Barthes goes back in time, he says, and tries to find "the truth of the face I had loved." He settles not on a recent photograph showing his mother near death, or in her final years, but rather on one of her at age five. Why was this? "During her illness, I nursed her, held the bowl of tea she liked because it was easier to drink from than a cup; she had become my little girl, uniting for me with that essential child she was in her first photograph." Barthes reasons that despite his childlessness, he has "engendered" his mother by caring for her during her illness. The photograph of the mother that leads Barthes back into lost time is one that readers will not see. The absent face, in a book illustrated by photographs, is replaced by the narrative Barthes substitutes of his own mothering of his dying mother—taking care of his mother, as if she were his little girl.

In *A Woman's Story* Annie Ernaux laments her mother's descent into the mental and physical deterioration caused by Alzheimer's disease. "I didn't want her to become a little girl again, somehow she didn't have the 'right.'" But later, when her mother is living in a nursing home, the reversal produced by second childhood becomes acceptable; it becomes the only possible social mode of relation. "She was always hungry," Ernaux writes, "all her energy had been concentrated around her mouth. She liked being kissed and would purse her lips in an attempt at mimicry. She was a little girl who would never grow up. I brought her chocolate and pastries, which I cut up into little pieces and fed to her." The daughter needed to cherish her mother/daughter, "needed to feed her, to touch her and to hear her." When your parent becomes a child who will never grow up, you cope with your pain by converting it to nurturance. If you can.

Images of adults caring for other adults who have become *like children* are of course moving. The narrative of care seems to satisfy some deep ethical sense about what connects generations; its social dimensions tend to vanish into the natural. You give, and what you give is returned. That's the way it's meant to work. In *And when did you last see your father?* British poet Blake Morrison, who is a father himself, watches his father die. "And I sit there breathing heavily, his hand in my hand, wondering if he, being the patriarch he was, ever changed a nappy of mine, and wondering if this might be a definition of what it is to be grown up—not changing your child's nappy but changing your parent's." Changing your parents, a fable for our times. Baby boomers shopping for adult diapers.

For a while after my mother's death I would go to the opera with my father in my mother's place. In the beginning, I loved being dressed up with my father at the opera; playing at being my mother, wearing her black velvet cape and her pearl choker. Music went directly to my father's emotional center. There was nothing intellectual or even of the true amateur about his delight. Isn't that beautiful, he would sigh, whatever the performance. And he would weep with abandon. As my father's disease progressed, however, it became harder and harder to get him to the scene of his pleasure. When he could no longer climb the stairs of the bus, I would shove him bodily into taxis (the drivers would always look away, as if they feared contamination). Intermission was taken up rushing him to the bathroom and back into his seat in the middle of the row, zipped up. Soon going to the opera became a major family production, punctuated by the humiliation of decline: wet pants, drooling face. But my father would not consider attending in a wheelchair, admit his infirmity. "Why not listen to it on the radio," my sister urged. Finally, my father reluctantly agreed that we should cancel the coveted center orchestra seats maintained over two decades, emblem of my parents' life together as a successful middle-class couple in New York.

When your parent becomes your child, the desire to requite is not the only feeling that is stirred; nor is all parental love freely given. The need to care for a frail or ailing parent is not always met with the beauty of the ethical, the gestures of the domestic sublime. "At the same time as I am her advocate," Mary Gordon writes in "My Mother Is Speaking from the Desert," she also is her mother's adversary. "I want to scream at her and say, 'How can you allow this to go on?' It makes me want to end her life. At the same time I want to sit in her lap and say, 'Don't you understand that I'm your child and a child shouldn't have to do this?'" Sometimes we are just exhausted by the effort of being there, occupying our rightful place, paying our dues as dutiful daughters or sons. "You had obligations, and you had to fulfill them," David Denby writes in "Queen Lear." But when his mother died, he admits, his "tears were produced as much by relief as by sorrow." Sometimes we can't separate relief from sorrow, resentment from love.

How do we put the memory of the dead on paper? There is a strange and necessary tension between what is documented and what is remembered, and that tension between these two modes of accounting for the past is part of what makes these works affecting and interesting. In the second volume of *Maus*, subtitled *And Here My Troubles Began*, Art asks his father about the Jews who played in the orchestra at Auschwitz (a scene that he says is "very well documented"). Vladek replies that he remembers "only marching, not any orchestras." He was there. How could there have been an orchestra? Art draws against—or in visual dialogue with—Vladek's memory by showing him marching past the orchestra in his striped prison garb, looking straight ahead while the orchestra plays in plain view of *Maus*'s readers. Yes, there was an orchestra; no, Vladek didn't remember it. Document and memory are both true, even if they are at odds with each other. But the child's version ultimately prevails, incorporating the failures of memory in a new narrative of the past. Susan Cheever describes reading a letter addressed to her father, left lying around, in which the letter writer explains that "although he was very fond of my father, he could not accept his physical affection." She puts the letter away without registering the message. She recalls the *scene* of reading the letter, she says, but "it wasn't until after my father died and I read his journals that I remembered what the letter meant."

The biography of a parent is always an act of remembering, and like all effects of memory, vulnerable to omission and distortion. (Doubly so, when two people—or more—remember their relation both separately and together. Do our sisters and brothers really have the same parents?) The actual coordinates of the map of feeling on which these family plots are located forever escape documentation. And yet those feelings *are* history, alive in the present tense of recollection. What makes these books so powerful as documents is the emotional record they offer of the auto/biographer at work as the scribe of memory, condemned to reconstruct the other in the face of loss—alone.

When writers engage in autobiographical acts they signal on the simplest level a desire to be read according to the expectations of autobiography as a "true story." Readers choosing their pleasure among the many forms of autobiographical performances demonstrate a reciprocal desire for this truth. That encounter is what French critic Philippe Lejeune has called "the autobiographical pact." The commitment to telling the truth and the desire to read it holds whether or not the truth in question can be verified. What matters is this bond between writer and reader. "The reader doesn't need to know this," Rousseau explains early in his *Confessions*, "but *I* need to tell him." The reader browsing in the nonfiction section of the bookstore seems to need that need. (The compulsion to tell is especially acute in these accounts for which parental death supplies the dominant perspective; and it finds expression in the impulse to exactness characteristic of illness narratives.)

More generally these memoirs that tell another's story turn to and include materials that Dutch historian Jacques Presser has called "egodocuments," a term he invented during his research on the Holocaust: "those documents [diaries, memoirs, letters, scrapbooks] in which an ego—the self—intentionally reveals or conceals itself." These documents are the work of survivors; and they reappear, reintegrated, in the art of the survivors' children. The use of diaries, oral testimony, interviews with relatives and friends, letters, and snapshots, like Barthes's photograph of his mother at age five, all contribute to the effect of a form that asks to be taken for the truth: at face value. These memoirs forcefully move readers to contemplate what is on each one's horizon: the death of a parent, and then one's own death. We may not respond sympathetically (sympathy is not required by the pact), but we are no less implicated.

Toward the end of his memoir, Blake Morrison worries about the figure he cuts as a middle-aged orphan. "I've become a death bore. I embarrass people at dinner parties with my morbidity. I used to think," he writes, "the world divided between those who have children and those who don't; now I think it divides between those who've lost a parent and those whose parents are still alive." After the death of parents, it's hard not to become a death bore. Sometimes, it's the only story we can tell. And sometimes things start to go better with our parents when they are dead. In an interview on National Public Radio, answering a listener's question about what—beyond

Maus—went on between him and his father, Spiegelman said that "getting the story *was* the relationship." Outside that, there was nothing much. "The process," he explained, "gave me a relationship." A relationship, he concluded, that was "improved by his death and by doing the book." When we write about the dead we write them into our lives, put them in a place from which we can move on.

When I was a beginning teacher, it fell to me in a required course devoted to the Greeks and the Romans to teach Herodotus's *Histories*. The students, mainly sophomores, read the *Histories* as part of a "great books" curriculum—masterpieces of European literature, as the phrase went. In an early section of the *Histories*, Croesus, the richest man on earth, receives the visit of Solon, the wisest man of Athens. Croesus asks Solon to tell him who is the happiest man he has ever seen. Solon gives examples that make no sense to Croesus, since the stories bear on the death of the subjects in question. To a bewildered Croesus, who had expected to find himself at the top of Solon's list, Solon explains: Until a man is dead, and we know the manner of his death, "keep the word 'happy' in reserve. Till then, he is not happy, but only lucky." When I witnessed the death of my parents many years later, the passage came back to me—along with my deafness to its meaning. I thought when I was young that everything lay ahead and that my parents would live forever—as they were, as we were. If I thought about their death, which I sometimes did, longing to be free of their hold over me, I never imagined *how* they would die. I certainly never imagined what happened: that in their own terms (which were not, of course, Solon's) they would die wretchedly; and that I would bear helpless witness to their undignified demise. Look to the end, Solon advised. But of course we can't look to our own, singular ends; we need literature for that. The knowledge of our parents' end, however, especially if we are called upon to provide intimate care, is instructive. Viewing an aged parent's naked form not only conjures a living image of one's ultimate fate; it brings home the facts of a shared, ineluctable physical bond. This end, which we cannot help joining, is not always, of course, a scene of prolonged agony. In some ways, the sudden death of a parent produces an even greater shock. This inexplicable occurrence shatters our confidence in some clear partition between the living and the dead. Lack of causality, Paul Auster writes in *The Invention of Solitude*, brings us "so close to the invisible boundary between life and death that we no longer know which side we're on." It's not easy to know which side we are on, when we are always on both. The boundary line is invisible. Shocking or expected, traumatic or uneventful ("she died in her sleep"), the death of a parent in the end sends us back to ourselves. If they are mortal, so are we.

In imagining the future—what would I be when I finally grew up—it had never occurred to me that my mother's death would leave me in charge of my father. That I, Ms. Oedipus, would at last have my father to myself, but that he would not be the good father of my childhood: Daddy. So in the end, though for quite different reasons, I was relieved when he died too. The morning of his death, the home aide called to say that my father kept trying to crawl out of the hospital bed he then slept in and that this was dangerous. I arranged for railings to be delivered that day. Later, just as I was dressing to go out to dinner, a neighbor who had been visiting my father called to say that he had made a funny sound (she imitated a gurgle) and that she thought it was all over. She had announced his passing, as she called it, so many times before—"come quickly, he's going fast"—that my first reaction was skepticism, or was it actually denial tinged with annoyance: Again? But when I arrived at the apartment twenty minutes later, heart pounding, my father had already started to turn a waxy yellow. He had died with his hand grasped around the brand-new bars of his bed, trying to pull himself up.

At the end of the third volume of her memoirs, *Force of Circumstance*, Simone de Beauvoir makes a remark that got her into a lot of trouble. Looking back at her life at age fifty-six, Beauvoir writes: "The promises have all been kept. And yet, turning an incredulous gaze towards that young and credulous girl, I realize with stupor how much I was gypped." The sentence puzzled many readers. But according to Beauvoir's biographer Deirdre Bair, the young woman with whom Beauvoir subsequently remade her life, Sylvie le Bon, seems to have "instinctively grasped" its meaning. Beauvoir's mother falls ill in the same year—1963—that these volumes of the memoir are published. What did Beauvoir mean by being "gypped"? A few pages before this ambiguous pronouncement Beauvoir describes her preoccupation with death and the horror that the sight of her face in the mirror inspires in her. The despondency of these pages today would be labeled depression, a woman's panic at the prospect of aging, the end of desiring—and being desired. But perhaps in these pages written *before* her mother's death Beauvoir imagines a form of disillusionment that can become the grounds for a life beyond the illusion of youth and plot. "There is no future," British psychoanalyst Adam Phillips remarks, "in repetition."

Thank You and Goodnight, a feature film that Jan Oxenberg calls her "docu-fantasy," starts out as a sophisticated home movie about a grandmother who is dying of cancer. Oxenberg films her grandmother as though she were making a documentary, shot in the hospital and at home. But she also creates cardboard characters—including one of herself—who coexist with family members, with stories of their own. They wander through surreal tunnels and get shot like rockets into other spaces and other times. Toward the end of the movie, the cutout self goes to therapy sessions in Jan's place to talk about her emotions. She feels immobilized by grief after her grandmother's death. Over shots of the granddaughter's prostrate form, the therapist's words echo like a mantra of recovery. "You have to close a door to open a door." Autobiography's house is constructed around a long hallway. Along the darkened corridor, a series of doors to the rooms of our lives open and close. It's surprisingly difficult to keep a door closed.

At a Thanksgiving dinner a few years ago, my aunt Evelyn, who has become famously forgetful, took me by surprise. "How are your parents?" she asked. Thinking I had not understood her question (I was dumbfounded), she added helpfully, naming them, "You know, Mollie and Lou." Mollie and Lou?! "Yes, I know," I replied, wondering whether to continue, "They're dead. Mollie died right after Al." (Al was my mother's brother.) "Oh, that's right," she agreed cheerfully, and then asked about my sister. For a moment, I confess, caught by the simplicity of my aunt's query, I wasn't sure myself. When *are* our parents dead?

With my sister, Ronna, in Riverside Park, New York, 1948.

2

CHILDLESS CHILDREN:
BODIES AND BETRAYAL

Ladies and gentlemen, my mother is
dying. You say, "Everyone's mother dies."
I bow to you, smile. Ladies, gentlemen,
my mother is dying. She has cancer.
HONOR MOORE, "Mourning Pictures"

"What am I going to do without him?"
"Write about him. That's what you have to do."
PAUL MONETTE, Borrowed Time: An AIDS Memoir

Writing about despair and confusion, even jotting down telegraphic
shards in my diary, always feels like a small gesture toward clarity
and hope. Writing anything in those moments seems to arrest the
free fall of anxiety I find so paralyzing. At a particularly low point in
my father's decline I wrote an essay that I called "My Father's
Penis." Although its pretext was the feminist discussion of the great
penis/phallus question (how can you tell the difference, or can
you?), its stakes were personal: my attempt to make sense of a life
that had stopped, or so it seemed to me, making sense. A lawyer and
intellectual (self-styled), my father could no longer read or write, no
more than he could get himself to and from the bathroom on time,
or sometimes at all. When I first read Philip Roth's *Patrimony* in
early 1991, my father had died and I was still living out his death as a
kind of daily dullness. I felt that I joined some piece of Roth's desire
to account for the experience of living with and through a father's
death. "A writer," Roland Barthes perversely declared in *The Pleasure of the Text*, talking (metaphorically) about the power of language

in modern writing, "is someone who plays with his mother's body." A writer, we could also say prosaically, is someone who takes notes while his father is dying. Or hers.

Roth isn't the first contemporary author to make autobiographical literature out of a parent's intimate suffering. In *A Very Easy Death* Simone de Beauvoir detailed the unfolding drama of her mother's death from cancer. I read Beauvoir's memoir before my mother's death from cancer, Roth's in the aftermath of my father's losing battle with Parkinson's. But books and deaths rewrite each other. When I revisit my father's last years, scenes from *Patrimony* become part of my home movie. When I think about what my mother's death meant to me, *A Very Easy Death* supplies a guide to the maze of emotional contradictions I still get lost in. But for me, deeper claims link these two memoirs, whose authors are both childless. The biography of a dying parent written by an author without a child can make autobiography a surprisingly painful journey. Writing about these books now as a reader without a child, I read, perhaps too autobiographically, looking for the effects of that story—between the lines.

Roth writes *The Facts: A Novelist's Autobiography* between his mother's death and his father's illness. As if rehearsing for *Patrimony*, he previews the filial persona of its writer. He makes fun of that version of himself through Nathan Zuckerman, the character of his own invention to whom he has sent the manuscript for advice about publication. "You find yourself bowled over, at the verge of tears with your feelings for this eighty-six-year-old man. This is the incredible drama," Zuckerman sarcastically remarks, "that nearly all of us encounter in relation to our families." By choosing *Patrimony* as his title, Roth aims for the universal dimensions of a father's legacy that Zuckerman predictably mocks. He also makes it the province of Jewish American sons. "Your Jewish readers," Zuckerman concludes, "are finally going to glean from this what they've wanted to hear from you for three decades. That your parents had a good son who loved them."

The good son. As the book's reviewers unfailingly pointed out, *Patrimony* takes its title from a scene in which Herman Roth is convalescing at his son's house in Connecticut. Having been constipated for several days following a hospital stay during which he has undergone a painful biopsy for a brain tumor, the father suddenly loses control of his bowels, dramatically soiling himself and the bathroom in the process: "I beshat myself," he explains. After cleaning up his father's body, the son warily confronts the side effects of paternal disarray:

> The bathroom looked as though some spiteful thug had left his calling card after having robbed the house. As my father was tended to and he was what counted, I would just as soon have nailed the door shut and forgotten that bathroom forever. "It's like writing a book," I thought— "I have no idea where to begin."

Although *Patrimony* doesn't begin here, the memoir is inseparable from this scene in the bathroom. To shut the door on the bathroom would mean not only *not* writing the book but forgetting that writing in some way always begins just there, in the spectacular but nonetheless ordinary mess of human life. So a writer has to remember the bathroom and return there in memory because that is where the material is. And there is a reward for going back into the room to finish the job:

> You clean up your father's shit because it has to be cleaned up, but in the aftermath of cleaning it up, everything that's there to feel is felt as it never was before. It wasn't the first time that I'd understood this either: once you sidestep disgust and ignore nausea and plunge past those phobias that are fortified like taboos, there's an awful lot of life to cherish. . . .
>
> And *why* this was right and as it should be couldn't have been plainer to me, now that the job was done. So *that* was the patrimony. And not because cleaning it up was symbolic of something else but because it wasn't, because it was nothing less or more than the lived reality that it was.
>
> There was my patrimony: not the money, not the tefillin, not the shaving mug, but the shit.

This is Roth's double paradox: Patrimony is not what is preserved but what is returned, not getting but giving. Patrimony sounds metaphorical but it's literal: what you see is what you get. Not because it was "symbolic of something else but because it wasn't." The point of *this* patrimony is its "lived reality." But can the lived reality of cleaning up your father's shit ever be detached from what it symbolizes? Roth's patrimony comes to mean reversing the flow of care between generations; returning, in some sense, the unreturnable, the incommensurability of parental devotion—symbolically.

As Philip watches over his father's bath, he finds it "gratifying to be able to requite somewhat by sitting on the lid of the toilet overseeing him as he kicked his legs up and down like a baby in a bassinet." Requital. Repayment. Not quite Aeneas carrying Anchises on his back as they flee burning Troy. Something less epic, more domestic. "Philip is like a mother to me," Herman Roth explains to the companion of his final years. Overhearing the conversation, the son is surprised by his father's choice of words: "I would have thought he'd say 'like a father to me.'" When Philip draws his father a bath, he remembers his mother's gesture of testing the temperature of the water for him with her elbow. The son is to his father as the mother was to her son. Musing about the aptness of the description, the son wonders why he is surprised. After all, it was the father who had taught him about language, by example. "He *was* the vernacular, unpoetic and expressive and point-blank." Like a mother to me. Still, the father's homely prose (the oddly archaic cadences of "beshat" notwithstanding) must pass through the son's literature.

If the act of cleaning up your father's shit isn't symbolic, memorializing the act necessarily is. Beyond the shit, *Patrimony* is largely about the lines of force that structure relations within the family plot. It's also about the ways those lines sometimes give way to permeable borders between mothers and fathers, mothers and sons, fathers and sons, and lead to skirmishes at the borders. Being like a mother, for instance, is also a child's pleasure in moving to a new, less vulnerable place in the family plot. Playing house, you are the one in control. When a childless son finds himself in his mother's place, he gets to play the parent he'll never be.

I hated cleaning up my father's shit, even though I only had to do it once. I thought that it was his fault, and technically it was. Frustrated by the con-

stipation brought on by the medication for Parkinson's disease and desper-
ate for a result, my father would overdose on laxatives. When in the course
of his illness it fell to me to clean up the mess—I found him one day stand-
ing in the passageway leading from his bedroom to the bathroom, immobi-
lized by the dimensions of the disaster—I was overcome both by the reality
and the "symbolism" of the event. The scene of this once elegant man splat-
tered with shit was unspeakable for both of us: his guilt and shame, my
horror and blame; his helplessness, my efficiency. Having to clean up the
shit felt like the remains of his power over me—his refusal, until the situ-
ation had reached crisis proportions, to let me hire someone to live in the
apartment with him and care for him properly. So yes, in that sense, there
was my patrimony, but for me the caretaking felt like a mockery of the
maternal. Like those pop art cartoons: "(Sigh) I wanted to have a baby, not
marry one!" I didn't want my father to be my baby. I didn't want to be
"like a mother" to him. And I was sick of Being a Good Daughter (though
I of course reveled in it as well). Mostly I thought that this was the culmi-
nation of all the shit his illness made me put up with. Taking shit: his con-
stant complaining, the endless tasks of running another household, the
white panic at being responsible for another life. Being like a son.

Cleaning up my father's shit shocked me into imagining the end of my
own life: Who would clean up after me? Who would be like a mother to
me?

After the accident, while helping Herman bathe, Philip observes his
father's penis: "It looked pretty serviceable. Stouter around, I notice,
than my own. 'Good for him,' I thought. 'If it gave some pleasure to
him and my mother, all the better.'" Comparing penises, measuring
the distance between the child's view and the adult's, Roth recalls
seeing his father's penis when he "was a small boy," when he used to
think "it was quite big." Looking at his father in the tub, it turns out
that he "had been right." A glance at a father's penis produces a
glimpse of a boy's future. "I remember how big it seemed when I
was a child at the swimming baths," Blake Morrison reminisces in
his memoir about his father's death. He recalls the thrill of identification. I looked forward to being an adult so I could have one that
big too. I think how as adult heterosexual males," he continues, "we

rarely see each other's penises and never see each other's erections—
least of all our fathers' erections—and I catch myself grieving that
he may never have an erection again. Then I think how embarrassing these thoughts are." Among the unanticipated effects of witnessing a parent's bodily decline are these embarrassing thoughts.
Children experience the sight of their parents' genitals in a double
chronology: both through childhood eyes and adult revision. The
child's unequal perspective survives in the adult's: as big as, not so
big. There's a peculiar plangency in the realization that the childhood gap has closed. That one is like one's parents in kind. Not so
different. Maybe not different at all. This comparability is both con-
soling and intolerable. We discover our fundamental likeness under
the pressure of the end. And then it's gone.

Roth doesn't just glance at his father's penis, he memorizes it:

> I looked at it intently, as though for the very first time, and waited on
> the thoughts. But there weren't any more, except my reminding myself
> to fix it in my memory for when he was dead. It might prevent him
> from becoming ethereally attenuated as the years went by. "I must
> remember accurately," I told myself, "remember everything accurately
> so that when he is gone I can re-create the father who created me." *You
> must not forget anything.*

Unlike the first scene in the bathroom, which leads backwards to
connection, contemplating the father's penis here rehearses future
separation and death: The father's penis stands in for the father as a
body (his physical and generative presence—"the father who created me") but also as the father's law. The Father speaks the voice of
authority: *You must not forget anything.* (These become the last words
of the memoir.) The commandment underlying all the others. Jews
are asked to remember and to not forget; part of what you remember has to do with where you come from. The literal and figurative
body. The penis is also the place in which Jewish genealogy gets
marked on the male body. A son is circumcised like his fathers
before him. Roth works backwards in memory to the Father.

Patrimony gets written in the space between two contradictory
injunctions: not to forget and not to tell. When Philip puts Herman

to bed for a nap after his accident, he promises his father that he won't "tell the children" (Roth's nephews) or his wife: "'Nobody,' I said. 'Don't worry about it. It could have happened to anyone.'" Not telling. Roth, the biographer of his father, knowingly runs the risk of betrayal. For a writer, especially a Jewish writer, not forgetting anything entails putting memory into language. (It's a form of covenant with major Old Testament antecedents, starting with Moses.) But that compulsion to record and bear witness collides with another biblical injunction—the one that forbids looking upon the father naked (as Ham discovers Noah lying famously drunk in his tent, and by telling his brothers, earns the father's curse). By including the plea for paternal privacy in his violation of it, Roth makes clear what side he has to be on. To separate from the other, father or mother, requires the enactment of one's own difference; the more likeness is asserted, the more difference is displayed. In this sense, betrayal—as an act of differentiation: there are two of us—seems to come with the territory of the family memoir. This is where I come from but not what I am.

When I was growing up, my father wore what we used to call string pajamas. Actually, I remember only the bottom part of the pajamas, which as their name might suggest, tied with a string at the waist. (On top he wore a ribbed sleeveless undershirt that tucked into the pajama bottoms.) The pajamas, made of a thin cotton fabric, were a droopy affair; they tended to bag at the knees and shift position at the waist with every movement. The string, meant to hold the pajamas up, was also meant to keep the fly—just a slit opening at the front—closed. But the fly resisted closure and defined itself by the meaningful hint of a gap.

As my father wandered through the apartment in the early mornings, performing his domestic rituals (bringing my mother her coffee in bed, making my sister and me breakfast, shaving), the gap never failed to catch my eye. As I watched him pass from room to room (drinking his coffee and watering the plants) in a circular slow motion repertoried in our family codes by the Yiddish trope of draying, I worried about what lay behind the flap: something important, dark, maybe verging on purple, probably soft and floppy, and . . . hairy. I don't think I wanted to see it—"it" had no name in my ruminations—but there was a peculiar way in which its mysterious daily existence behind the slit in the pajamas loomed large in my prepubescent imagination.

More than forty years after the scene of these memories, I find myself again, as a middle-aged therapized intellectual, thinking about my father's penis. Living alone in the same apartment after my mother's death, my father shuffles through the room draying. Boxer shorts have replaced the string pajamas of his preferred at-home garb, but my sense of the darkness has changed. I've touched my father's penis. One day when his fingers had grown so rigid that he couldn't, as he put it, "snare" his penis, he wanted to get up and go to the bathroom. It was late and I wanted to go home. So looking and not looking, I fished his penis out from behind the fly of his shorts and stuck it in the urinal. It felt soft and a little clammy.

Penis. Phallus. Show and tell. Shit and tell.

In the prologue to *The Facts*, Roth describes his father "trying to die"—though not actually ill as he is in *Patrimony*—and locates his primary identity as a son and a writer, his signature, under his father's style and name.

> His resolute dutifulness, his relentless industriousness, his unreasoning obstinacy and harsh resentments, his illusions, his innocence, his allegiances, his fears were to constitute the original mold for the American, Jew, citizen, man, even for the writer, I would become . . . in the embroilment with the buffeting world, my history still takes its spin from beginning as his Roth.

The mother gives birth to the boy ("To be at all is to be her Philip"), but the writer is born of his father. Beginning, he says in *The Facts*, as his Roth. Retelling his stories:

> It wasn't exactly the first time I was hearing these stories. Narrative is the form that his knowledge takes, and his repertoire has never been large: family, family, family, Newark, Newark, Newark, Jew, Jew, Jew. Somewhat like mine.

What separates a writer from his beginnings? Roth the son from Roth the father?

As an act of transmission, patrimony requires both connection and distance between generations. In the same way, the subject of the memoir about a father by a son is necessarily double—father *and* son. The work of memorialization occurs in the space of that relation, within the family plot. So despite the son's conscious will to identification, the writer lays out the gap that cannot be bridged: "the poignant abyss between our fathers and us and that they themselves broke their backs to give us." What separates fathers who are the sons of immigrants from sons whose fathers are American sons is a world of language and education. "Encouraging us to be so smart and such *yeshiva buchers*," Roth recalls, "they little knew how they were equipping us to leave them isolated and uncomprehending in the face of all our forceful babble." Studying not at home in the shtetl but off at college, being smart, leads the sons away from and not back home. This is something the sons can feel guilty, make literature, about.

> Every course I took and paper I wrote was expanding the mental divide that had been growing wider and wider between us since I had prematurely entered high school at twelve, just about the age when he had left school for good to help support his immigrant parents and all their children. Yet for many months there was nothing my reasonable self could do to shake off the sense of merging with him that overcame me in the library and in the classroom and at my dormitory desk, the impassioned, if crazy, conviction that I was somehow inhabited by him and quickening his intellect right along with mine.

This reflection takes place before the biopsy and before the scene that gives rise to the naming of the book, the exposition of paternal estate. Patrimony is both about what you inherit by birth and what comes to you after a father's death. Patrimony haunts identity (you can't get rid of the parent in your head) and is changed by its effects (the person the child becomes by virtue of the parent in the head). With the death of a parent, especially a parent with whom one has identified, one continues to hear—overhear—the dead voice in the head. You write what your father speaks, just as you eat what your parents cook.

If the father supplies the original material—the mold, the stories, the knowledge of narrative—the son puts it into writing, marking his difference. And that marking has an edge. In the course of developing the portrait of his father's character, Roth publishes one of his father's letters to Philip's brother, Sandy. The vernacular constellates the page with its idiosyncratic spelling, punctuation, and grammar. Roth excerpts bits from other letters written by Herman, but this father-son letter is replicated down to the last detail, perhaps because it constitutes a signed self-portrait. The father's self-representation as Hocker confirms the son's characterization of him, in which an authorial Roth reaches for a recognizable, if not entirely appealing, type glossed for the goyim. The writer supplies the dictionary entry in a parenthesis: "Hock: a Yiddishism that in this context means to badger, to bludgeon, to hammer with warnings and edicts and pleas—in short, to drill a hole in somebody's head with words."

> Why do I continue, hocking? I realize its a pain in the ass, but if its people I *care for* I will try to cure, even if they object or wont diceplin/disaplin themselves I including myselve. I have many battles with my conscience, but I fight my wronge thoughts. *I care* for people in *my way.*
>
> Please excuse the spelling and writing. I was never a good writer but now its worse, I don't *see so good*
>   The Hocker, Misnomer
>   It should be the carer
>   Love
>   Dad.
>
> I will always continue to
> Hock and Care. Thats me
> to people I care
> for

Even in a work that takes vulnerability as its theme, there's something troubling about finding this letter on display. Comparing penis size works gallantly at the author's expense, the catalogue of the shit's effects genially produces authorial benefit (what a good son). Both push at the limits of readerly tolerance but publishing the letter ups the ante: this is after all a *writer's* patrimony, and this broken prose, his father's language. The vernacular spelled out. Roth worries in *The Facts* about the problem, as he puts it, of exposing others: "While writing, when I began to feel increasingly squeamish about confessing intimate affairs of mine to *everybody*, I went back and changed the real names of some of those with whom I'd been involved, as well as a few identifying details." The squeamishness about confessing others did not seem to be a guiding principle in *Patrimony*; of course now the (significant) others are dead.

You could argue that publishing the letter recognizes Herman's capacity for self-knowledge and guarantees his posterity—as Philip Roth's father. And yet exposing the vulnerability of an uneducated father, putting the private letter into the public domain, also betrays his biographer: The outing of illiteracy documents the son's need to maintain the distance separating him from the father with whom as an adolescent he briefly feared he might merge. In these memoirs of a dead or dying parent the ambitious wish of the writer is irreducibly alive. Violate the spirit of the injunction—you must not forget anything—by taking it to the letter. Reminding himself, reminding us, that who he is, what he is, is before all the writer.

After holding my father's penis in my hand, for a while I went around thinking that I would never again confuse penis and phallus, boasting that I had transcended the theoretical confusion. Phallus was the way my father could terrify me when I was an adolescent: throwing me across the room in a blind rage, knocking me down in the elevator for staying out late one night with my college boyfriend. Phallus was tearing the pages out of the typewriter because I hadn't left wide enough margins on my term paper; forcing me to break a date with the cab driver who had picked me up in London on my first trip to Europe (but Daddy, he's Jewish, the son of a cantor!). Penis was that dark-veined, heavy thing lying there against strangely elongated, even darker balls, hanging between emaciated but still elegant thighs. Penis made problems for me, but they were finally prosaic, unencumbered by symbolic meanings.

.   .   .

Parables of the literal. *Patrimony* is the narrative—Roth calls it "a true story"—of a father's dying and of what the legacy of that event turns out to mean for him. More than inheriting the father's stories or cleaning up the shit, patrimony seems to mean reconstituting through memory what *connects* generations. A framed photograph of the Roth men on vacation, posed in a row of descending size, occupies the center of the cover; the image separates the name Roth from the title of the memoir. Wearing a strap undershirt, Herman, looking straight ahead, is standing behind his sons, his arms hanging at his sides: not touching. In front of him is Sandy, the older brother, with his hands resting on the shoulders of his little brother. Low man on the totem pole, Philip, age four, looks out of the portrait, away from the camera, mischievously (working on being sardonic). Roth reads the portrait from the bottom up: "The three of us rise upward to form a V, my two tiny sandals its pointed base, and the width of my father's solid shoulders . . . the letter's two impressive serifs. . . . There we are, the male line, unimpaired and happy, ascending from nascency to maturity!"

Mrs. Roth stands outside the frame of this celebration of masculine solidarity. Maybe Mom's taking the picture. But where is the mother in this text? Philip's mother is invoked in counterpoint to his father in *The Facts*:

> The link to my father was never so voluptuously tangible as the colossal bond to my mother's flesh, whose metamorphosed incarnation was a sleek black sealskin coat into which I, the younger, the privileged, the pampered papoose, blissfully wormed myself whenever my father chauffeured us home to New Jersey on a winter Sunday from our semiannual excursion to Radio City Music Hall and Manhattan's Chinatown: the unnameable animal-me bearing her dead father's name, the protoplasm-me, boy-baby, and body-burrower-in-training, joined by every nerve ending to her smile and her sealskin coat. . . .

Mother is body, father is story. But what is the mother's story? There's a tribute to her sensitivity and to her extraordinary housekeeping skills, but as a woman she remains a cipher. At the beginning of *Patrimony*, when Roth is driving out to New Jersey to deliver the bad news to his father about his brain tumor, he makes a wrong turn and ends up in the cemetery where his mother is buried. He comments on the mistaken itinerary the following day, a trip he does not regret having taken: "I wondered if my satisfaction didn't come down to the fact that the cemetery visit was *narratively* right: paradoxically, it had the feel of an event *not* entirely random and unpredictable and, in that way at least, offered a sort of strange relief from the impact of all that was frighteningly unforeseen." Roth missed his mother's death, which recurs as a mystifying blank. There's a story of how it happened. Roth can retell it only in his father's terms. His father's death he lives—for the reader at least— in the pages we have before us, in the book about what cannot be foreseen but what must be narrated. Visiting his mother's grave confirms the piece of the story he already has: that his mother loved him, and that his attachment to that love is comforting. In *Colored People*, Henry Louis Gates, Jr., expands on that feeling of unambiguous bereavement. "I wanted the whole world to know my mama's death and her glory while alive. I wanted to cry and cry and cry, so I could tell her how sorry I was for not being a good enough son," Gates writes about his pain at his mother's funeral. "I wanted her to know that I could have tried to do more, I could have tried to understand better, I could have come home more. I wanted her to know that I had tried and that I loved her like life itself, and that I would miss her now that she was gone. I wanted to be sad in that dark, holy place, and I wanted that sadness to last." But *that* sadness doesn't last. It gets taken up into writing.

In the shadow of your father's death, you visit your mother's grave. This looks forward to the end that is in sight and looks back on what's already lost. It's easier to deal with what's done.

The story of *Patrimony* is the unfolding narrative of illness and death; it is also the record of a discovery. The Roth persona, while recognizable from his earlier, more extravagant self-fictions, tries on the part of a regular human being, albeit a literate one. "I find that while visiting a grave one has thoughts that are more or less anybody's thoughts and, leaving aside the matter of eloquence, don't differ much from Hamlet's contemplating the skull of Yorick." Of course the matter of eloquence is never really left aside here (no more than Hamlet's); this is after all a writer's memoir—but a writer who embraces cultural commonplaces. "What cemeteries prove, at least to people like me, is not that the dead are present but that they are gone. They are gone, and, as yet, we aren't. This is fundamental and, however unacceptable, grasped easily enough." Losing a father turns out to mean feeling ordinary things, wanting ordinary things—the objects, for instance, that represent him: that attach to, derive from, his body (this is the dictionary definition of patrimony, before the shit). The banalities of autobiography. What's yours, what's your father's, your grandfather's.

Roth explains that after his mother's death, when he was discussing his father's affairs, he had renounced his share of the estate. Now that his father's death looms, the gesture suddenly seems as wrong in its effects as it was generous in intention: "I felt crushed for having done it: naive and foolish and crushed." This realization comes at almost the dead center of the book.

> I wanted the money because it was his money and I was his son and I had a right to my share, and I wanted it because it was, if not an authentic chunk of his hardworking hide, something like the embodiment of all that he had to overcome or outlasted. . . .
>
> Didn't I think I deserved it? Did I consider my brother and his children more deserving inheritors than I, perhaps because my brother, by having given him grandchildren, was more legitimately a father's heir than was the son who had been childless? . . . Just where had this impulse to cast off my right of inheritance come from, and how could it have so easily overwhelmed expectations that I now belatedly discovered a son was *entitled* to have?
>
> But this had happened to me more than once in my life: I had refused to allow convention to determine my conduct, only to learn, after I'd gone my own way, that my bedrock feelings were sometimes more conventional than my sense of unswerving moral imperative.

On what grounds do we inherit from our parents? We inherit because we are their children. What we inherit is meant to be handed down to our children. Grandchildren are what children give back to their parents; it's a system of exchange. What happens to entitlement when this chain is broken, when the child breaks the chain by not having children? *Perhaps*, Roth says, perhaps being childless made him think he had no rights. The critic's classic move is to track the places where the autobiographer seems blind to the screen of his own self-disclosure; the cannier the writer, the greater the desire on the part of the critic to uncover this spot. I want to lean briefly on the "perhaps" of Roth's childlessness as a possible explanation for this regretted gesture of self-repudiation, and on the understanding Roth offers here of his motives.

While thematically testimony to a parent's dying, *Patrimony* and *A Very Easy Death* also tell the story of a coming to terms with one's own conventionality (being like everyone else) in the face of that common experience. The power of this realization derives in part from finding oneself confronted as an adult—Roth and Beauvoir are in their mid-fifties at the time—with the contingency, somehow avoided until then, of the physical bond between generations. A parental body in decline reminds us of the founding ordinariness of life that is lodged in the body itself. This is a knowledge which not having children, and not living the implacable domesticity that daily care for them *as bodies* entails, manages to forestall for a very long time. The demands of the dying parent's body mark the end of deferral. But paradoxically, this revelation turns back on itself and exposes conventionality's ultimate condition: the plot of generations. Parents, children, parents, children, grandparents.

Because she spent the months of her illness at home, my mother's dying lacked the high technodrama of the hospital; and since my father managed her care, I was spared its daily spectacle. My distance from the scene of physical detail and relative normality of the household routine allowed me to experience her dying as though we were in another era, indeed another genre. I in fact kept hoping for a deathbed confession, in which I would learn the truth of her life. I was sure there was an unhappy secret that would explain why I always felt something was fundamentally wrong, or missing, or unsatisfying. I desperately wanted her to admit that she would have been happier having a career in which she made enormous amounts of money, rather than having spent her life trying to harangue my father into being more aggressive in the marketplace and pretending, even though she actually had worked part-time for many years (as a substitute teacher in the local elementary school), that she was a woman of leisure, in addition, of course, to being a full-time housewife and mother. That would have satisfied my own analysis of her misspent life: Beauvoir passed through the grid of Betty Friedan, "the feminine mystique," the privileged dilemma of postwar white American middle-class women. Every time she told me she had a "rich, full life" (tennis, yoga, Europe, the opera), I concluded that she meant just the opposite. Maybe she was faking it. That might begin to account for the hostility she periodically displayed toward my life, in all points opposite to hers: a trajectory of jobs and degrees that finally had begun to resemble a career, but also a series of unhappy relationships (and no children)—the price, no doubt, of a sexual freedom she once confessed to imagining as that of a whore (in her mind, it seemed, my boyfriends had metamorphosed into a line of faceless men waiting for their turn).

Patrimony ends on a dream about the rule of generations, or rather on a waking reading of its significance.

> In the morning I realized that he had been alluding to this book, which, in keeping with the unseemliness of my profession, I had been writing all the while he was ill and dying. The dream was telling me that, if not in my books or in my life, at least in my dreams I would live perennially as his little son, with the conscience of a little son, just as he would remain alive there not only as my father but as *the* father, sitting in judgment on whatever I do.
>
> You must not forget anything.

It bothers some readers that Roth admits, almost in passing, to have been writing his memoir while his father was dying. The word Roth uses to characterize this lapse in taste, we have seen, is "unseemliness." But if, as his dream tells him, appropriating a father's suffering for his own professional requirements is wrong, it is at the same time the thing that gives the suffering its due. For if the ultimate commandment of filiality is to not forget, then the will to record answers to a higher law. But who decides what should be recorded? What weighs heavier in the balance, a father's desire for privacy or a son's need to tell, to reauthor himself? Perhaps, to grow up. You know you're still a little son when you believe in the father's law and break it. That's the story patriarchy (patrimony) keeps alive. ("As the story of his father's death," Adam Phillips points out in an essay on the memoir, "*Patrimony* is the first of Roth's books his father would never read.")

Canonically, autobiography charts a journey out, the emergence from the zones of everyone's obscurity into a singular public identity: leaving home, becoming a writer (the story told in *The Facts*, for instance, or through Beauvoir's multivolumed memoirs, of being *unlike* everyone else). For these writers the autobiographical act embedded in the portrayal of the other folds back on itself into homeliness, dailiness, the commonest places. But not only. For if the memoir is bound to the deployment of these recovered values (one's bedrock feelings), writers both embrace them and remain elsewhere in the acts of authoring their books.

Tossing off a characteristic aphorism, Phillips remarks apropos of *Patrimony* that for Roth, "what you inherit is what you have to get rid of." How do you get rid of what you have inherited when there's no one in line to receive it? For whom do you write when no one comes after you? What you inherit is what you have to get rid of. Roth seems to be suggesting that if in the logic of patrimony what you give back is what you receive, then his book is a kind of posthumous grandchild, a bequest of memory. Herman gave Philip his father Sender's shaving mug—the one thing *he* wanted from *his* father. What will happen to it when Philip dies? Like the book, dedicated to "our family, the living and the dead," Sender's shaving mug must go to someone, since it can't be returned—to sender.

> Ladies and gentleman, one last time: My mother's dying. I haven't got another.
> HONOR MOORE, "Mourning Pictures"

Like Philip Roth, Simone de Beauvoir composed her death memoir well into a distinguished writing career and as an adult child who by her notoriety had shocked but certainly also impressed her parents.

A Very Easy Death opens with Beauvoir in Rome learning by a phone call from a good friend in Paris that her mother has had an accident. For both writers the narrative of decline involves a pulling back from the displacements of a certain chosen glamour to the physical demands of a parent's failing body. Beauvoir and Roth are forced to think about home, even if they don't literally return there. Beauvoir's account of her mother's illness—from the apparent simplicity of a broken hip to the hopeless complexities of misdiagnosed intestinal cancer—is rooted in the scene of the clinic, and the drama of the "easy" death unfolds from the confines of the hospital bed. Her mother's history, which this enforced return to the maternal orbit seems to require, is a biography constructed from the sight of that body in pain.

By calling his father's story *Patrimony*, Roth highlights the task of cleaning up his father's shit. As we saw earlier, he also insists on our taking this act in without any symbolic coin, but the language works against it: In our vernacular, being full of shit, like taking shit, is a matter of words. What cleaning up a parent's shit makes shockingly visible is our need for some things to remain a matter of words. When words like shit become lived realities, the relation between words and things is inverted. Cleaning up shit requires not thinking of the task as taking shit. On the contrary. Real shit has a lesson to offer about our attachment to our parents' bodies, especially when we rely on the integrity of their bodies for our ideas about who we are. Real shit brings home our need for this unchanging relation, which is experienced both in real time—and in memory. If we have the slightest doubt about these body boundaries, the spectacle of the parental body out of control removes it.

We can read Beauvoir's encounter with those boundaries in a scene that offers an asymmetrical counterpoint to the second bathroom episode in which Roth compares penis proportions with his father. For Beauvoir the comparable revelation—but are son/father, mother/daughter alignments every truly analogous?—comes early in the medical narrative. One day, while Beauvoir is visiting her mother in the clinic, the physical therapist, in reaching for her mother's leg, uncovers her mother's lower body:

Maman had an open nightdress on and she did not mind that her wrinkled belly, criss-crossed with tiny lines, and her bald pubis showed. "I no longer have any sort of shame," she observed in a surprised voice.

"You are perfectly right not to have any," I said. But I turned away and gazed fixedly into the garden. The sight of my mother's genitals had jarred me. No body existed less for me: none existed more. As a child I had loved it dearly; as an adolescent it had filled me with an uneasy repulsion: all this was perfectly in the ordinary course of things and it seemed reasonable to me that her body should retain its dual nature, that it should be both repugnant and holy—a taboo. But for all that, I was astonished at the violence of my distress. My mother's indifferent acquiescence made it worse: she was abandoning the exigencies and prohibitions that had oppressed her all her life long and I approved of her doing so. Only this body, suddenly reduced by her capitulation to being a body and nothing more, hardly differed at all from a corpse. . . .

There is no easy female equivalent of patrimony, since matrimony leads away from the mother and since it's always less clear what, under patriarchy, a daughter can inherit from her mother, let alone pass on or return. What does the scene of a mother's bodily suffering mean to a daughter's idea of herself? "Why," Beauvoir asks in the final chapter of this painful portrait, "did my mother's death shake me so deeply?" This is not a question Roth asks himself, since the answer seems self-evident to him: I have lived this loss as my father's son. A father who is not myself, but like myself. For daughters the loss touches on the problem of analogy itself. How am I like? Am I, in fact—my mother? For daughters separation from the mother emerges from a founding confusion of boundaries. Anne Sexton condenses the dilemma in "Housewife": "A woman *is* her mother. That's the main thing."

Except for the effects of the chemotherapy, my mother's cancer was almost invisible. When she died, I found myself alone with her corpse. Unembarrassed by her dead-eyed stare, I carefully examined the body that had fascinated me all my life and that now lay open to my inspection. Although she was never really fat, my mother had weighed more than she wanted to and was constantly developing ingenious strategies for circumventing calories while indulging a sweet tooth (her "ice-cream soda," for instance, a child-hood favorite from Grandpa Miller's summer candy store, reconstituted with seltzer, coffee, and ice-milk). After two months of not eating, my mother had at last melted into the size she longed to be. Despite its obvious frailty, her newly slim body, thoroughly exercised over a lifetime of fitness avant la lettre (we found a colored poster in a drawer naming her the "most popular member" at the 92nd Street Y), was unnervingly youthful. And her face revealed the bone structure she had always maintained was the true source of beauty. My mother was particularly gratified by the con-fession of a friend's husband (a doctor who happened to see patients in the hospital where she had her chemo) that he hadn't realized how beautiful she was—until she was dying. So I guess you could say that my mother died finally looking the way she had wished to live: beautiful and thin.

Roth admires the hardiness of his father's penis, but Beauvoir is repelled by the sight of her mother's genitals. When she sees her mother's bald pubis, she averts her gaze. Seeing her mother embod-ied "as a woman" ruptures any conventional bonds of female conti-nuity; to be of woman born is not necessarily a comfort. She looks, and looks away. Unlike Roth, Beauvoir does not compare herself to her mother *as a woman*. Beauvoir's life project refused the entire legacy of female identity. She revolted against the concept of Woman and the price of embodiment. For Beauvoir, being embod-ied was women's unenviable fate. If one is not born, rather one becomes a woman, Beauvoir sought to escape the ground of that becoming. By not having children and by living the life of the mind, a life shared with Sartre, Beauvoir tried to outplay the laws of gen-der. So when the author of *The Second Sex* looks at her mother, she begins by a disavowal. She looks away. Her own belly, pubic hair, genitals are not sites of complicity and identification with her mother as another woman. The points of connection—and discon-nection—are those of the spirit, sometimes the spirit of the body. Beauvoir approves of her mother's lack of shame.

Beauvoir's vision of her mother, not unlike her *Second Sex* analysis of woman in Western culture, is dual: cherished and reviled, sacred

and repugnant. The illness revives that double bind, the figures of
the two mothers:

> The "Maman darling" of the days when I was ten can no longer be
> told from the inimical woman who oppressed my adolescence; I wept
> for both of them when I wept for my old mother. I thought I had made
> up my mind about our failure and accepted it; but its sadness comes
> back to my heart. There are photographs of both of us, taken at about
> the same time: I am eighteen, she is nearly forty. Today I could almost
> be her mother and the grandmother of that sad-eyed girl. I am so
> sorry for them—for me because I am so young and I understand noth-
> ing; for her because her future is closed and she has never understood
> anything. But I would not know how to advise them. It was not in my
> power to wipe out the unhappinesses in her childhood that con-
> demned Maman to make me unhappy and to suffer in her turn for
> having done so. For if she embittered several years of my life, I cer-
> tainly paid her back though I did not set out to do so.

The two photographs embody the divide that separates the two
women, mother and daughter, but also splits each pair in two: the
good mother and the bad, the dutiful daughter and the rebellious
one. Their story is one of failed connections between generations of
women. Even in the present tense of writing, incomprehension remains. I would not know how to advise them: Two women who
don't understand each other, who are destined as women to miss
each other. Each one longs for the other's recognition; each withholds it because of her history, her childhood unhappiness. *A Very
Easy Death* is in part the drama of how that recognition belatedly
takes place: two women giving up their war, a war not of their own
making.

In *Patrimony* the photo chosen to represent the "male line" is a
single photo, in which the dominant image is that of visible connection and jubilation, V for Victory. What Roth comes to see—to
want to see—in his father's illness is how much joins them still: "I
could even believe (or make myself believe) that our lives only
seemed to have filtered through time, that everything was actually
happening simultaneously, that I was as much back in Bradley with
him towering over me as here in Elizabeth with him all but broken

at my feet." In the end, *Patrimony* comes to bear witness to how, after all, as Zuckerman put it in *The Facts*, Philip was a good son who loved his parents. Roth remains devoted to the father he has monumentalized. Although, as we have seen, the lesson of Roth's patrimony seems dependent on the assumption of resemblance (how like his father he is, how much they are made of the same stuff), this will to likeness reads almost as a form of atonement for the betrayal of the letter. Almost. Publishing a facsimile of the letter in its stunning inadequacy is a disavowal of their shared identity. Nonetheless, it's the photograph of family resemblance that comes on the jacket cover to illustrate the title of patrimony, and Roth describes his desire to "join the two fathers and make them one," the father of memory in the picture and the father now "all but broken" at his feet.

Patrimony's cover announces a nostalgia for connection and identification alien to Beauvoir. She chooses not one photograph but two, two images of division to represent her relation to her mother (her sister does not figure in the scene: not the female line). In a rare play on maternal identity, Beauvoir imagines herself as her mother's mother and grandmother to herself. But this is not a happy solution: even in her fantasized wisdom, she is powerless to make the images speak to each other. What is the female equivalent of patrimony? French feminist Luce Irigaray stages it this way in an imaginary dialogue between mother and daughter called "And the One Doesn't Stir without the Other": "With your milk, mother, I swallowed ice." Nurturance does not come naturally. When Beauvoir looks back over her childhood and adolescence, she sees disconnection and repudiation. Getting even. Settling scores.

There's a color photograph that captures the state of the war between my mother and me in the mid-sixties. We are standing in an airport—Orly, I think, or maybe Heathrow. My parents have visited me in Europe, where I have been living for several years despite their desire for me to return home. I am saying good-bye to my mother and, judging from the expression on my face, she is telling me something I don't want to hear. I am standing in the light, wearing dark glasses and a scarf arranged in a kind of turban. The light dramatizes the planes in my face, and if it weren't for the snarl

*that distorts my mouth, this would be a flattering portrait. My mother is
silhouetted in the shadow. She is about the age I am today. She is looking at
me and I can see on her face, then, the collapse along the jawline I now read
on mine. We have the same fragile profile, separated by a generation. I am
holding a gloved hand across my body, she is holding a purse against hers.
In the photograph, the two women look at each other across their war. We
are alone fixed in our struggle.*

*My father likes this picture, which he had enlarged from a color slide
and framed. It's a good picture, he says.*

If Roth longs to close the gap between his father and his self,
Beauvoir needs the distance of the gap to survive. Beauvoir, whose
strength (but also weakness) as a writer has always been her absolute
determination to see the truth—in this case her belief that family
sentiment is based largely on ideologies of repression—resists the
lure of filial piety. It is true that by bringing her internal conflicts to
light, the illness produces a mother Simone finds it easier to love:
"She had an animal passion for life which was the source of her
courage and which, once she was conscious of the weight of her
body, brought her towards truth." But if Beauvoir feels more comfortable with this vision of her mother—a mother made more
attractive (less *other*) by the intensity of her physical desire for life
(the "truth")—like Roth she is finally moved beyond the expectations of her daughterly performance by the facts of her mother's
broken and defeated body: "My despair escaped from my control:
someone other than myself was weeping in me." Who is this *someone
other* in herself? Who am I, faced with my mother's suffering?

One piece of that puzzle of identity can be found within the question *A Very Easy Death* asks without ever answering: "Why did my
mother's death shake me so deeply?" Building on Freud, critic
Kathleen Woodward argues that while the death of a father is the
most significant event in a man's life, "the most excruciating test to
which a woman can be put is the loss of her child." And she concludes, provocatively: "Beauvoir suffers here as if from the death of
the child she never had." What does it mean to experience the loss
of your mother as though it were the loss of a child you never had?

This is not a figure of substitution—the parent in the place of the child—but a redoubling: losing the parent after losing the child one never had. The imaginary mourning attaches with extra poignancy to the present drama; imaginary loss comes to rework the real one. The double loss requires a double mourning. It's at least in part because of this imaginary loss (never admitted: *I* imagine it in Beauvoir's place), I think, that Beauvoir has so much trouble answering her own question.

This notion of a double mourning also surfaces in *Patrimony*. The writer undergoes an emergency quintuple bypass in the course of his father's illness and suddenly invokes the complexity of familial bonds across genders. Imagining that he is giving suck to "his own newborn heart," he feels himself "androgynously partaking of the most delirious maternal joy." Roth revels in his transgendered status: "I was as near to being the double of my own nurturing mother," he explains, "as . . . I had come to feeling myself *transposed*, interchangeable with . . . my failing father." For Roth, gleefully changing places within the familial scenario *as if* in a fiction of his own design, nurturance is not threatening but cause for narcissistic jubilation: the ultimate fantasy of self-creation. For Beauvoir, however, the breakdown of roles engendered by compulsory caretaking produces an unexpected panic. Metaphors of nurturance, thoroughly denounced (perhaps autobiographically) in *The Second Sex*, are lined with violence in the death memoir where—repelled by her mother's helplessness and the pleasure her mother seemed to take in being dependent—Beauvoir nonetheless respects the ethics of requital. The collapse of the body and the decorum of its functions marks the divide and the passage of the child into the role of protector:

> Mademoiselle Leblon and a red-haired nurse tried to put her on to a bed-pan; she cried out; seeing her raw flesh and the harsh gleam of the metal, I had the impression that they were setting her down on knifeedges. The two women urged her, pulled her about, and the redhaired nurse was rough with her; Maman cried out, her body tense with pain.
> "Ah! Leave her alone!" I said.
> I went out with the nurses. "It doesn't matter. Let her do it in her

bed."

"But it is so humiliating," protested Mademoiselle Leblon. "Patients cannot bear it."

"And she will be soaked," said the red-head. "It is very bad for her bed-sores."

"You can change the clothes at once," I said.

I went back to Maman. . . . "You don't have to bother about a bed-pan. They will change the sheets—there's no sort of difficulty about it."

"Yes," she replied. And with a frown and a look of determination on her face she said, as though she were uttering a challenge, "The dead certainly do it in their beds."

From this perspective we may understand Beauvoir's image of some-one other than herself weeping inside her as the mother she never wanted to be weeping for the child she said she never wanted to have. Perhaps what Herman expresses in "Philip is like a mother to me" is also that fantasized maternity: the other in himself Philip might have wanted to be. Perhaps, finally, threaded through these memoirs of another's dying is the story of a double loss: a childless writer confronted with the story of what didn't happen.

Beyond the lost mother or father, and the end of parents alto-gether, the memoirs invoke a style of emotional being in the world gone forever. They record the traces of a double mourning: *as if* for the child one never had, as if for all one would never be. Because the story of generations is already moot, parent and child remain locked forever in nostalgia's embrace for all they both were and never were to each other. There is in this version no second chance.

Unlike Roth's passion for identification (maternal or paternal) in *Patrimony*, Beauvoir's aim in *A Very Easy Death* is to keep the story of her disconnection from her mother straight: "Generally speaking I thought of her with no particular feeling." But her experience fails to sustain that conviction.

I talked to Sartre about my mother's mouth as I had seen it that morn-ing and about everything I had interpreted in it . . . that did not want to admit its existence. And he told me that my own mouth was not obeying me any more: I had put Maman's mouth on my own face and

in spite of myself, I copied its movements. Her whole person, her
whole being, was concentrated there, and compassion wrung my heart.

My mother, myself. It's hard to tell the difference when your body
defies the divide. The truth implicit in that *involuntary* knowledge of
what binds bodies together in spite of themselves is what drives the
narrative and undermines its authorial will to know. We may not be,
the sight of a parent's suffering teaches us, who we think we are. As
Beauvoir concluded about the photographs, the pact that linked the
two women was one that involved a compulsion, if not a commitment, to pay the other back. She bears witness to the knot of
recrimination that mounts upwards in the chain of generations: negative requital. If her mother, because of *her* mother, condemned
Simone to unhappiness, Simone, by her own account, certainly paid
her back. But when her *body* takes over, retribution ceases.

Nonetheless, by virtue of Beauvoir's autobiographical *style* (which
embodies her ideological astringency), that convulsive experience of
compassion is never completely severed from her will to erase its
effects. So Beauvoir writes in the memoir's final pages:

> In spite of appearances, even when I was holding Maman's hand, I was
> not with her—I was lying to her. Because she had always been de-
> ceived, gulled, I found this ultimate deception revolting. I was making
> myself an accomplice of that fate which was so misusing her. Yet at the
> same time in every cell of my body I joined in her refusal, in her rebel-
> lion: and it was also because of that that her defeat overwhelmed me.

Throughout the dying the relationship lives on in Beauvoir "in its
double aspect—a subjection that I loved and hated." That double
feeling is embedded in the deepest folds of the memorial project.
Beauvoir writes:

> I had grown very fond of this dying woman. As we talked in the half-
> darkness I assuaged an old unhappiness; I was renewing the dialogue
> that had been broken off during my adolescence and that our differ-
> ences and our likenesses had never allowed us to take up again. And
> the early tenderness that I had thought dead forever came to life

again, since it had become possible for it to slip into simple words and actions.

This tenderness, which Beauvoir sees as being released by the simplification of her mother's life and language through illness, in turn releases Beauvoir's compassion and produces her dedication. Although her judgment of her mother's life *as a life* remains harsh, it is neither uncomprehending nor unforgiving; and the daughter, devastated by the childlike voice of her mother's suffering *as a person*, is saddened, moved, and shaken by the misery she is unable to relieve. "How completely alone she was! I touched her, I talked to her; but it was impossible to enter into her suffering." Nonetheless, despite the emergence of this unexpected complicity and Beauvoir's *physical* identification with the maternal body—"And I too had a cancer eating into me—the lesson moves *out* from her mother and herself to the universal always close to Beauvoir's heart. "Everyone must die: but for each of us death is an accident, and even if we know it and consent to it, an unjustifiable violation."

In the hospital it was war between my father's penis and the doctors' discourse. I wanted to stand in as phallus for his debilitated penis. I represented the rights of his wounded body against their authority to determine the course of his life and I fought their wish for him to live, despite his entire system's disarray (my wish for him?). Maybe now, lacking the penis, I'd have my chance at the phallus. When I read one day on my father's chart in the intensive-care unit, "Responds only to pain," I found it hard to share the doctor's jubilation over the signs of life dotting the monitor over his respirator. "What do you want me to do," she hissed at me over the network of tubes mapping his body, "kill your father?"

Given Beauvoir's vision of the world, the death pedagogy of *A Very Easy Death* reaches for generalization and, in some important ways, resists the lessons of Roth, who in *Patrimony* comes to embrace the truths of conventional wisdom. Beauvoir learns instead that the clichés of human destiny—"He is certainly of an age to die"—are false. "I too made use of this cliché," Beauvoir writes, "and that when I was referring to my mother. I did not understand that one might sincerely weep for a relative, a grandfather aged seventy and more. . . . We are all mortal." Her mother's agony teaches her that the commonplaces fail to render another reality: the feelings of attachment that live on in us, whatever we think we may have done with them. These feelings are as involuntary as the suffering that produces them. Beauvoir's new understanding is the knowledge that typically drives the memoir of a dying other. Like Roth's discovery that he wanted, was entitled, to inherit from his father, Beauvoir's discovery of the lie behind the commonplace—"of an age to die"— comes as a shock. For an intellectual like Beauvoir, who thought she had solved the mind/body problem through voluntary acts of self-transformation, when the truth masked by cliché emerges in her face it throws her entire system out of control.

Both *Patrimony* and *A Very Easy Death* chart in detail the story of bodies that no longer know themselves and whose subjects have lost control over their own narratives:

> I looked at her. She was there, present, conscious, and completely unaware of the story she was living through. Not to know what is happening underneath one's skin is normal enough. But for her the outside of her body was unknown—her wounded abdomen, her fistula, the filth that issued from it, the blueness of her skin, the liquid oozed out of her pores; she could not explore it with her paralyzed hands, and when they treated her and dressed her wound her head was thrown back. She had not asked for a mirror again: her dying face did not exist for her. She rested and dreamed, infinitely far removed from her rotting flesh, her ears filled with the sound of our lies; her whole person was concentrated upon one passionate hope—getting well.

This peculiarly *inhabited* dispossession, in part created by the plots of a technology not dependent upon human subjects, is perhaps the cause for the strangeness of these accounts, their modernity and their familiarity. What is the appropriate way to write and then to read the signs of bodies pushed to their limits by science, age, and

illness? Beauvoir offers one model. As Elaine Marks puts it, "repli-
cating her position as an intimate observer and helpless witness,"
Beauvoir creates a space that allows readers to both identify with
and distance themselves from the experience.

*About a week before she slips into the coma, my mother tells me she wants
to see me alone. I am incredibly excited because our story is finally taking
the turn I've been hoping for. I arrive from my office and go to sit with her
in the bedroom. My mother is very weak; she has refused all medication but
the doctor thinks she is not in pain because the cancer has reached her
brain. Still, I have been summoned clearly enough to her bedside. After a
brief pause, she tells me that my father was not a satisfactory lover. Not
that he wasn't "ardent," just incompetent. I am floored by this statement,
since my mother has always maintained in a tone that both intimidated
and demoralized me (the whore) that a woman could experience true physical satisfaction only in marriage and that she was satisfied (the "rich, full
life"). But if this new, deathbed version of things were true, it would
explain, on the one hand, the bedrock of resentment that seemed to support
the monument of her marriage, and on the other, the strange hilarity with
which she reported her best friend Barbara's accounts of "PEs" (premature
ejaculators). The conversation goes no further. I, who was always ready to
debate her authority, for once remain speechless.*

When Roth contemplates his father's penis, "the one bodily part
that didn't look at all old," he deduces his mother's pleasure, conventionally, from its size. "If it gave some pleasure to him and my
mother, all the better." In that sense, re-creation of the father (the
son's authorial project) entails re-membering him: seeing his father's
penis anew, revitalizing its claims to masculinity. Beauvoir looks at
her mother's naked belly, written over with the marks of age, and
looks away as though it were no longer a sexual body; she gladly
goes out, at the nurse's request, to buy her nightdresses that won't
irritate bedsores. But later in the memoir, when the daughter
returns to her mother's body, now beyond shame, through the narrative she has constructed of her parents' marriage, she returns to

the time of that body's sexual life in order to imagine the mother's desire, the scene of a pleasure that Roth, bonding with his father, takes for granted.

> Her senses had grown demanding; at thirty-five in the prime of her life, she was no longer allowed to satisfy them. She went on sleeping beside the man whom she loved, and who almost never made love to her any more. . . .
> When after my father's death, Aunt Germaine hinted that he had not been an ideal husband, Maman snubbed her fiercely. "He always made me very happy." And certainly that was what she always told herself.

"I do not blame my father," Beauvoir declares at the threshold of this dark maternal biography. Does this mean she blames her mother or just that she forgives her father? I try to sort this out. How does a daughter know what her mother felt like sleeping next to a man she loved and who no longer desired her? How can a daughter know what her mother never admitted to herself?

Thinking about his parents' marriage, Roth recalls a conversation with his mother a year before her death in which she told him that she was thinking of getting a divorce, that she was fed up with Herman's interrupting her, shutting her up in public. Roth observes how little a boy brought up as a "good boy in a secure, well-ordered home—and simultaneously as a good girl" knows about the "inmost intertwining of mother and father's life together." As a "good girl" (or boy), Roth guesses nothing about what goes on between his parents; as a grown son, however, he assumes that his mother's pleasure is subsumed by his father's penis. Beauvoir worries as a daughter about the curtailment of her mother's pleasure, just as her mother worries about the expansion of hers. Beauvoir explains how little her mother really knew about her daughter's life; she hoped Simone was a "good girl" but ultimately was forced by her books not only to recognize that this was an illusion but also to tolerate her disillusionment because, as a successful author, the former good girl had become the "family's breadwinner—her son, as it were." Son or daughter, mother or father, without turning to fiction, there is no secure knowledge of the other's sexuality, even—or especially—when it's confessed.

The biography of the dying other is as much about what we can't know as what we do. In its final moments, the declining parental body insists on the necessity of separation, on the limits of the truth.

In the penultimate chapter of her memoir, Beauvoir speculates about what would have happened if, on the one hand, her mother's cancer had been diagnosed earlier, and if, on the other, the doctors hadn't operated (they had promised not to) and kept her alive for another month of pain. The reprieve produced by the useless operation, Beauvoir concludes, resulted in an unexpected benefit for her: being saved ("or almost saved") from remorse. This period allowed Beauvoir and her sister, by "the peace that our being there gave her, and by the victories gained over fear and pain," to redeem in their economy the neglect they had visited on their mother during the last few years of her life. Still, the lesson for Beauvoir remains that of loneliness: "The misfortune is that although everyone must come to this, each experiences the adventure in solitude. We never left Maman during those last days which she confused with convalescence and yet we were profoundly separated from her." The consciousness of a double solitude and the tenderness restored by this adventure of death underwrite perhaps the only but hardly minor irony of this searing book (probably Beauvoir's greatest literary work) marked in its title, the easiness of dying: "A hard task, dying, when one loves life so much." Every easy death is never not also a hard death. "Dying is work," Roth writes in the last pages of *Patrimony*, "and he was a worker. Dying is horrible and my father was dying." Beauvoir's memoir ends on a generalization: "Everyone must die: but for each death is an accident"; Roth's on an injunction, ostensibly addressed to himself, but doubtless to the reader as well: "You must not forget anything." But what to do after the remembering?

Autobiography is often seen as the history of a becoming—attaining freedom, finding a voice, getting published—and an overcoming, of obstacles, crises, incapacities. Here the autobiographical narrative, by its focus on the failing other, provides the account of an undoing, an unbecoming. That's one side of the story. The other side of the story has to do with the gain offered by that loss.

It cannot be the accident of biography alone that the intense, ambiguous, and twenty-five-year friendship with Sylvie le Bon, a woman thirty years younger than Beauvoir, begins at this juncture in Beauvoir's life: "It was her mother's death that brought us together," Sylvie explained to Deirdre Bair. The two women always hotly denied that any maternal component on either side played a role in their relationship. "My own mother was quite enough for me, thank you," Beauvoir stated firmly. "And as for children, I knew from my own childhood that I did not want them. I had no vocation for such things." Sylvie le Bon is as clear. "Neither of us had any taste for motherhood or family ties," the younger woman asserted unequivo-cally. Nonetheless, Beauvoir legally adopted le Bon, making the younger woman her daughter and heir. Whatever the motives or pretexts—primarily the need for Sylvie to have legal responsibility for Beauvoir as the aging writer's health dramatically failed—the effect was to create a bequest that countered after the fact the *as if* of maternal loss (grieving *as if* for the child she never had). Instead, Beauvoir left behind, with a formidable literary legacy, a woman who resisted the plots of biological reproduction Beauvoir herself had refused in her life. Beauvoir invents Sylvie le Bon de Beauvoir, her literary executor, and creates a new story—whose truth remains veiled—of love between two women of different generations.

At this moment in my own narrative of remembering I find myself at a crossroads. I want to follow both paths: the one that connects me to Jews, the story of Jewish son Art Spiegelman (coming to grips with his father's— and dead mother's—story) and the one of childless daughter Carolyn K. Steedman (writing in the shadow of Simone de Beauvoir, about what ties her to her dead mother's anger). If I choose the Jewish connection, I break the thread that binds this daughter to her dead mother. If I choose childless-ness, I lose the Jews (although such choices are more easily made in a book than in life).

*No sooner do I choose—a meal at a restaurant, a paint color, a lover—
and the feeling rushes over me like a wave of nausea. I'm five years old and
I've made the wrong choice.*

*I remember this. I have been kept home from school, kindergarten,
because I've had my tonsils removed. I remember the ether, seeing "stars,"
going under, which I loved (still do). I wake up early one morning and
decide that I will go back to school. I open the maple dresser and choose a
yellow V-necked sleeveless vest that my mother has knitted. I deliberately
pick out the sweater, with its double stripe of mauve and hunter's green,
which I wear over a plain pleated skirt. I proudly march into my parents'
bedroom to announce my intention to go to school. My mother stops me at
the threshold: You can't wear plaid with stripes. How could I have failed to
know this obvious truth?*

*My therapists have always loved this story, my only childhood memory,
which I have told many times. Who says you can't wear plaid and stripes?
Why don't you have more confidence in your own opinion? Why, the more
philosophically inclined ask, do I think there is a single right choice? Why
do you feel you need to choose?*

*After my father's death, I found the sweater in a box of things my
mother had saved: a silver baby rattle with my birth date on it suspended
from a mother of pearl ring, a brown velvet muff, a poodle skirt from the
fifties, the sweater (with my name tag sewn in—*NANCY KIPNIS*). In the
home movie of 1946 I am wearing the sweater at the beach over a summer
frock; my sister is wearing the same outfit. Why did my mother save this
sweater? Was it an example of her handwork—like the poodle skirt with
her own appliqué? The perfectly matched and fully fashioned seams she
taught me to look for as the sign of a "good" sweater, not to mention the
sign of a good mother.*

*I chose—I still choose—my father over my mother. I chose—but did I
choose?—not to have a child. This book is haunted by the effects of choices
that aren't choices: who your parents are. So I go on to another story of
childlessness.*

With my mother at the Jersey shore,
summer 1942.

3

MOTHERS AND DAUGHTERS: THE PRICE OF SEPARATION

> The pain of separation from my breast was at least as
> sharp as the pain of separating from my mother. But I
> made it once before, so I know I can make it again.
>
> AUDRE LORDE, *The Cancer Journals*

> ... as we talked, our voices became one voice, and we
> were in complete union in every other way. What peace
> came over me then, for I could not see where she left off
> and I began, or where I left off and she began.
>
> JAMAICA KINCAID, "My Mother"

"Why did my mother's death shake me so deeply?" is the question
Simone de Beauvoir never fully answers in *A Very Easy Death*. And
yet the book's power to disturb comes directly from the mix of emotions stirred by that event. Perhaps the question supplies its own
answer. If the bond "between mother and daughter—essential, distorted, misused—is the great unwritten story," as Adrienne Rich
boldly declared in *Of Woman Born*, a mother's death does not release
its knots so easily. A mother's death may foreclose further twists of
the plot that links generations of women. But the mother's voice
continues to reverberate in the daughter's house of memory.

*My mother died on April 7. It was almost fifteen years ago. She had been
in a coma for several weeks, and finally her heart stopped beating. She died
of lung cancer that had spread to her bones, throughout her body. The odd
thing was that after a while she didn't seem to be in pain and had refused*

all medication. The night she died we went as usual to the Seder at her sister's house. "Why is this night different from all other nights?" is one of the questions ritually asked at the Seder. But no one volunteered the answer that would have fit that night. No one cried or even said anything. Maybe that was right. It was almost as though nothing was different, and in a way, nothing was. My mother had already left us behind with her body; the doctor said her brain had been "involved." The next day my father and I, like coconspirators, trudged through the snow left by a spring blizzard to the bank vault where I retrieved the jewelry she had left me in her will.

In his eulogy to a woman he had never met, the rabbi, counting the house, said it was a really good turnout, especially considering the weather.

Are our mothers ourselves? This is a question that feminists have asked in different ways with no little passion in every stage of feminist theory. The confusion of boundaries between mother and daughter has been seen as both desirable and terrifying, productive and destructive. Adrienne Rich famously analyzed this anxiety of resemblance as "matrophobia": the fear of *"becoming one's mother."* Rich defined the fear—now an article of faith in the feminist dictionary—this way: "matrophobia can be seen as a womanly splitting of the self, in the desire to become purged once and for all of our mother's bondage, to become individuated and free." The mother, Rich argued, "stands for the victim in ourselves, the unfree woman, the martyr. Our personalities seem dangerously to blur and overlap with our mothers'." In response to that overidentification, and wanting to resist the mother's power, the daughter strikes out against her mother for—but also against—herself. "In a desperate attempt to know where mother ends and daughter begins, we perform radical surgery." The harder it is to separate, the more desperate the need to cut ourselves off from the woman—in ourselves and in the mother—we can't bear to resemble.

What does a daughter want from a mother, what does a mother want from a daughter? One and the same thing: recognition. To see the other *for*—not *in*—herself. (You can't get your mother to see you if neither of you can tell the difference.) In making the case for the "intersubjective view" of human identity, psychoanalyst Jessica Benjamin emphasizes the need for a dialogic approach to relation, a recognition of "the other as a separate person who is like us yet distinct." But given the unequal relations of parent to child, can this exchange ever be symmetrical? Given the tenacious hold of the maternal figure Benjamin describes in "The Omnipotent Mother," the powerful image that dominates Western cultural scenarios of development, what are the chances of maintaining the fragile balance between what is like us and what is distinct without succumbing to violence on one side or the other? Perhaps if as daughters we resist what Benjamin calls the twin monsters of "adoration and dread," we might find "consolation for the inevitable disappointment of not being, or having, everything." If no one has everything, perhaps we all get to have something. Something almost magical, like a wand in a fairy tale that turns fantasies of disappearance—of loss—into stories of accommodation, even gain. When daughters write in the wake of a mother's death, their books portray the double task of separation—the inevitable tension, as Benjamin puts it, between "struggle for independence" and "confrontation with difference." They record the complex negotiations that construct the experience of "leaving and losing the other, even of death." Leaving home, leaving the mother behind, carrying on after her death— writing the mother, writing her death. The mother/daughter memoirs also show how a daughter's deepest ideas about a mother's body are inseparable from her ideas about herself. When as daughters we seek to create a portrait of our mothers, when we re-create our mothers' physical presence in our lives, our own shadow falls on the picture we take.

Annie Ernaux's *A Woman's Story* is a book about the decline and death of a mother who ran a café-grocery in the French provinces. Carolyn K. Steedman's *Landscape for a Good Woman: A Story of Two Lives* charts the childhood histories of a working-class mother and a daughter in postwar England. In these memoirs, a mother's death becomes the occasion for a reflection about the power of the mother's voice—her demands and desires—to shape a daughter's life. Like *A Very Easy Death*, these acts of memory bear witness to

the intricate and painful acts of separation that turn the daughters
into authors of their mothers' lives.

A Woman's Story opens on this minimalist frame:

> My mother died on Monday April 7 in the old people's home attached
> to the hospital at Pontoise, where I had installed her two years previ-
> ously. The nurse said over the phone: "Your mother passed away this
> morning, after breakfast." It was around ten o'clock. . . .

What is Ernaux trying to do in her memoir? "This book can be seen
as a literary venture," she explains, "to the extent that its purpose is
to find out the truth about my mother, a truth that can be conveyed
only by words. (Neither photographs, nor my own memories, nor
even the reminiscences of my family can bring me this truth.) And
yet, in a sense, I would like to remain a cut below literature." A
mother's death represents the end of a daughter's physical enmesh-
ment in her childhood world. "It was her voice, together with her
words, her hands, and her ways of moving and laughing, which
linked the woman I am to the child I once was. The last bond
between me and the world I come from has been severed." Through
an experiment in rewriting the past, *A Woman's Story* seeks to bridge
the gap between the missing maternal body and the daughter who
remains. This means neither identification nor repudiation, but
acknowledgment of a necessary distance: the space of writing.

Like Ernaux's elegiac meditation, Carolyn Steedman's memoir
opens with the scene of her mother's death, a prologue entitled
"Death of a Good Woman."

> She died like this. I didn't witness it. My niece told me this. She'd
> moved everything down into the kitchen: a single bed, the television,
> the calor-gas heater. She said it was to save fuel. The rest of the house
> was dark and shrouded. . . . She had cancer . . . talked to me about cur-
> ing it when I paid my first visit in nine years, two weeks before her
> death: my last visit. . . . She complained of pains, but wouldn't take the
> morphine tablets. It was pains everywhere, not in the lungs where the
> cancer was. It wasn't the cancer that killed: a blood clot travelled from

her leg and stopped her heart. Afterwards, the doctor said she'd been out of touch with reality. . . .

The prologue closes with eyewitness testimony. "Like this: she flung up her left arm over her head, pulled her knees up, looked out with an extraordinary surprise. She lived alone, she died alone: a working-class life, a working-class death."

The two memoirs lay bare the intimate ways in which working-class origins can inflect the stories of mother/daughter attachments in postwar France and England. Through the narrative of a childhood lived in the shadow of her mother's, Steedman stages "a drama of *class*." She writes, she says, for others *like her*, outsiders whose stories have not been told, "people in exile, the inhabitants of the long streets." If her narrative is effective, others "may start to use the autobiographical 'I,' and tell the stories of their life." Steedman describes the experience of reading collections of personal essays and memoirs and feeling painfully excluded from "these autobiographies of middle-class little-girlhood and womanhood," envious of insiders. When women friends protest—saying "but it was like that for me too, my childhood was like yours; my father was like that, my mother didn't want me"—they are missing the point. They live, Steedman maintains, "in a terrible exclusion, an exclusion from the experience of others that measures out their own central relationship to the culture." The storyteller positions herself as irretrievably separate and set off from this audience of other women, "friends"— feminists—who think they speak the same language. The effects of this exclusion cut two ways. You don't know us because you are the center from which, against which, the borders are defined, and you don't know it. I know you but am not of you.

As a reader who has lived a "middle-class little-girlhood," I find myself guilty as charged. Like Steedman I tend to define myself in my life against the desire, as she puts it, to reproduce, which she poses as the ground of the difference she shares with her mother: their "sense of exclusion, of being cut off from what others enjoy." But for me to insist autobiographically as a reader on resemblance—

I felt cut off too; I didn't want to mother, and my mother didn't either—would only seem to prove her point: I can't see that however similar those feelings may seem to me, the structures of our experiences are fundamentally different. And yet, *Landscape for a Good Woman* moves me because of the powerful ways in which it renders the maternal legacy that makes the daughter *not a mother*. Reading as a middle-class girl now grown up, I meet this unmothered daughter through a gesture of counteridentification. Yes, our childhoods are the site of our enduring difference. (The way we were.) And yet, despite her warnings, against her resistance, I read with her—reader to writer, writer to writer—when I read autobiographically, along her lines, as a woman who also lacked the desire to mother.

Between the two passages from "Death of a Good Woman" in which she evokes the final moments of her mother's death, Steedman recalls an episode from her childhood shortly after the birth of her baby sister. This experience of injustice underwrites her adversarial view of social relations. A social worker comes to inspect their home and declares, "This house isn't fit for a baby." Steedman describes her mother's reaction to the brutality of that judgment, her tears of rage and bitter courage, and then adds:

> And I? I will do everything and anything until the end of my days to stop anyone ever talking to me like that woman talked to my mother. It is in this place, this bare, curtainless bedroom that lies my secret and shameful defiance. I read a woman's book, meet such a woman at a party (a woman now, like me) and think quite deliberately as we talk: we are divided: a hundred years ago I'd have been cleaning your shoes. I know this and you don't.

The four-year-old bonds with her mother against the social worker: "We both watched the dumpy retreating figure of the health visitor through the curtainless windows." That scene shapes the pattern of future identifications—with the mother, against all others. Relived in the memoir, the health visitor has been reconfigured as a published intellectual or academic. This is a woman whose book Steedman will have read. A woman she puts into parenthesis, "now, like me." (I wonder autobiographically: Not like her then, am I like her now?) Reading her story, crossing the class divide through an identification with maternal rejection, I revisit my history.

"We are divided." My response pulls two ways at once in the two times of autobiography. As the daughter of American postwar middle-class parents (I would need to add New York Jewish professional middle-class parents), I am the enemy. But if we met at a party, Steedman and I, a middle-aged feminist intellectual ("a woman now, like me") who perhaps also took Simone de Beauvoir too seriously, or at least too uncritically, wouldn't this give us something to say to each other—despite our original class assignments?

Steedman's mother died in 1983. Two years later Steedman published an autobiographical self-portrait "Landscape for a Good Woman" in a collection entitled *Truth, Dare or Promise: Girls growing up in the 50s*. Like the other writers in the volume, Steedman focuses primarily on childhood, and the twenty-page self-narrative contains the kernel of the book she will publish four years later. In the contributor's note Steedman briefly describes her career as an intellectual and a writer; along with some personal information that would not be included in the longer work, she also supplies a snapshot of her three-year-old self taken with her mother. I read *Landscape for a Good Woman* a few years ago and wrote about it without having seen the earlier version. I now find myself in a perplexing situation: I know things I didn't know about Steedman when I discovered *Landscape* but that new knowledge is not part of my original experience nor will it be part of most readers' coming to the book for the first time. Does this matter? Wanting to leave the memoir its aesthetic and psychological integrity but also wanting to confront it with Steedman's other writings (her 1992 collection, *Past Tenses*, comments on the memoir as well), I've decided to return to both readings, before and after.

Steedman places her childhood at the center of her book, but that childhood of the postwar fifties makes sense to her only when seen through the lens of an earlier experience. "My mother's longing shaped my own childhood." The subtitle of the book, *A Story of Two Lives*, is to be taken literally. When Steedman reconstructs her childhood she passes it through her mother's, a biography which she authors. What about women who, like her mother, "refuse" to mother? Steedman wants to understand their singular story in general terms: "*how* the wish not to have a child might come to be produced in a little girl, or in a grown woman" and "what the refusal of a baby or a child is actually a refusal *of.*" There is also the kind of revolt that occurs *within* motherhood in a culture where "either socially or physiologically" women could not bodily refuse to bear children. This is how Steedman understands her mother's attitude: "Never have children dear, they ruin your life."

I cannot claim that I have *refused* to reproduce, since at various times in my life I flirted with the possibility and tried to conceive a child—strenuously, for two miserable years—in my early forties, at the borderlines of my fertility. Rather, by virtue of a tenacious ambivalence and treacherous propensity for deferral, I have not done so, and probably never really wanted to in the first place. ("Children aren't everything," my mother would say bitterly but also convincingly when I wondered if I would ever have a child.) For me, as for many women of my generation in the United States who modeled our identities on Beauvoir's famous split—babies *or* intellectual accomplishment—it might be more accurate to say that like Steedman we refused to reproduce *as women*, as though anatomy were our destiny instead of history, on schedule as though we had no say. Only then some of us changed our minds (or thought we did in a frenzy of belatedness) and it turned out that for many of us "nature" (or maybe it really was history) would have the last word after all.

There's a painful irony in the coexistence at the end of the twentieth century of a massive infertility which has given rise to dizzying adventures in reproductive techniques with the renewed challenges to women's reproductive rights. Choosing motherhood or refusing it has proven to be more complex than we feminists had bravely imagined in our consciousness-raising groups of the early seventies. *Our Bodies, Ourselves*, the title of one of the most important collective projects to emerge out of seventies feminism, nicely glosses the conviction of that moment: The comma, rather than the copula—

our bodies *are* our selves—underscored the determination that *we* would decide on what language best described the complicated relation between our body and our selves. We were not *just* our bodies, but we authorized ourselves to have the decisive role in deciphering their meaning and determining their circulation in the world. (The update of the volume, by the way, for women over thirty-five is called *Ourselves, Growing Older.* I guess without bodies. Which might actually be an improvement.) Whatever our respective singular and collective intents about reproduction, however, the effects— wished for or not—are shared. To be a childless adult (and to be straight) represents a peculiar form of marginality in a culture dependent on identities of generation. Steedman's story surprises, given the maternalism in and outside of contemporary feminism: the defiant tone of self-identification of a woman who has not had— says she never wanted to have—a child.

When I was a little girl I had a dollhouse which I loved with an intensity perhaps peculiar to urban children whose experience of space is an apartment and a shared bedroom. The dollhouse was a present on the only Christmas my sister and I succeeded in getting our guilty assimilationist parents to celebrate (no tree, of course, but stockings hanging from the mantelpiece of the nonworking fireplace); after that, we returned to the more parsimonious installments of Hanukkah. I played for hours on end with my white frame house and enlisted my mother's labor in the requirements of my scenarios. She made doll's clothes—tiny, knitted red snowsuits for my five (!) children. There was also a miniature tea set. I'm not sure I actually knew anyone who lived in a house (not to mention with five children), but it didn't seem strange at the time. Most of my playtime was spent either rearranging furniture or coming up with names: Cheryl, Beryl, and Meryl. I can't explain the rhyme. Maybe they were triplets. I don't remember actually doing anything with the girls, but I have always been able to remember those three names; maybe the other two were boys. I sometimes think that this failure of imagination— the children's reality was limited to the rooms they would occupy—actually may have something to do with my subsequent failure to conceive ("unexplained infertility").

I once revealed the existence of my imaginary children to a colleague. We had been plotting about job negotiations; he said, "So when you discuss salary, tell them all the kids are in college now, and you need more money." I laughed, of course, but it reminded me how abstract (oddly the word I want here is conceptual*) the idea of children or motherhood had always been for me: in my fantasy, the children never left their rooms; they certainly never grew up to go to college.*

Steedman recalls the stationary existence of her two imaginary children, Joan and Maureen, who lived in the flat with her in their blue and green gingham dresses: "I don't know what I did with them when I conjured them up," she writes, "but they were there, behind the mangle all through the summer and winter of 1950–51, as my mother carried my yet-to-be-born baby sister." Following British object-relations analyst D. W. Winnicott, Steedman takes the existence of these "fantasy children" as proof that she had received "good enough" mothering when she was a small child. In Steedman's reconstruction of her history, she had four years of this good-enough mothering—perhaps directly inspired by her mother's listening to Winnicott on the radio—and then "expulsion from the garden" with the birth of her baby sister.

Why didn't the fantasy children lead to a wish for real children? Why, moreover, did she not go on as had her sister (daughter of the same mother, but is it ever the same mother?) to produce children of her own? These are not questions Steedman answers. But here, close to the center of *Landscape for a Good Woman*, in a chapter called "Reproduction and Refusal," Steedman ties the wish for a child to a mimetic relation between the mother's and the daughter's body, and she explains the difficulty she had accepting her mother's adult female body as her destiny.

Steedman divides her view of her parents' bodies into zones above and below her waist—"I was extremely knowledgeable about breasts"—to the point of tasting breast milk as a four-year-old. She associates the symbolic cut between Eden and after with the breast feeding of her little sister: "It was with this most familiar part of my mother's body that I came to symbolize her ambivalence towards my existence. What came free could be given freely, like her milk: loving a baby costs very little." Steedman claims to not return the ambivalence personally; she doesn't seem to have experienced the massive "revulsion" from her mother's body that many women writers have described. She recalls her mother as "an attractive woman who kept her figure," yet admits to feeling a sense of "revulsion based on some obscure recognition of a difficulty, and ambivalence." The notion of revulsion is bound up with the *idea*, rather than the actual body of her future female self. "The distance and distaste of the girl child from what has produced her, and what she might become." The woman in her mother's body is what the daughter most fears becoming. "My refusal of my mother's body was," she writes, "a recognition of the problem that my own physical presence represented to her; at the same time it was a refusal of the inexorable nature of that difficulty, that it would go on like that, that I would become her, and come to reproduce the circumstances of our straitened unsatisfying life." Refusing a mother's body, as Beauvoir forcefully argued in *The Second Sex*, both is and isn't about its physical reality.

(Steedman seems to have assumed, as did Beauvoir and her younger sister, that to have children was necessarily—magical thinking—to replicate one's mother's life in the gender and number of one's children. And these horrid little girls would have the identical—negative—feelings about their mothers. Only their mothers were us. Unlike Beauvoir's sister, Steedman's sister decided to run the risk of being hated. In *Truth, Dare or Promise* we get a bit of detail: "My sister had her first baby at seventeen, her second nine years later. She's done it all by herself on social security. We're both daughters of the state, but she's poor and I'm not.")

There was no getting away from my mother's body. After a bath, she would emerge clothed simply in a towel: a white towel tied around her waist. She would often lie on top of the bed in the towel and read or work the crossword puzzle. When my sister and I were little, we would walk in on her during her bath; even much later, we would come barging in (her term) with a request, since in the tub she was almost always in a good mood. I remember thinking that she had a body like our saddle shoes, two-toned: tanned, freckled arms and legs from playing tennis, pale torso and white, pear-shaped breasts with erect, darkish pink nipples. The body I remember is not the half-submerged body of my childhood memories, though; it is the mother's body seen from my adolescence, the body I studied at twelve and thirteen as I waited for my own body to reveal its secrets.

Steedman makes the provocative claim that a "little girl's body, its neat containment, seems much more like that of a man, especially if she does not really know what lies between his legs." Her father's body, she asserts, "was in some way mine, and I was removed from my own as well as his." At a distance from the bodies of both her mother and her father, Steedman ends up in exile from a corporeal identity. (My body is *not* my self.)

This tentative identification with a father's body emerges in direct counterpoint to Adrienne Rich's famous account in *Of Woman Born* of seeing her parents' bodies when she was a girl. Rich maintains that the "first knowledge any woman has of warmth, nourishment, tenderness, security, sensuality, mutuality" comes from the mother and that this "earliest enwrapment of one female body with another" is the basis of a girl's connection to the world. To make her case for how gender identifications take root in family plots, in which a daughter transfers those feelings of maternal attachment to men, Rich turns to her own memories:

> I saw my own mother's menstrual blood before I saw my own. Hers was the first female body I ever looked at, to know what women were, what I was to be. I remember taking baths with her in the hot summers of early childhood, playing with her in the cool water. As a young girl I thought how beautiful she was. . . . In early adolescence I still glanced slyly at my mother's body, vaguely imagining: I too shall have breasts, full hips, hair between my thighs—whatever that meant to me then, and with all the ambivalence of such a thought. And there were other thoughts: I too shall marry, have children—but *not like her*. I shall find a way of doing it differently.
>
> My father's tense, narrow body did not seize my imagination, though authority and control ran through it like electric filaments. I

used to glimpse his penis dangling behind a loosely tied bathrobe. But I had understood very early that he and my mother were different.

This reminiscence, which opens the chapter "Motherhood and Daughterhood," allows Rich to explore the psychological ambivalence of these visions. The mother's body is like a map of possibility: you could follow its markers but still carve out your own path. Like her but not like her. A daughter, then a mother, but a daughter not reproducing her mother's existence. A biological continuum, not a social one. A mother's body but not her life; father's power but not his body. What do little girls not see when they look at their parents' bodies? How much can you really not know?

"Did your breasts always sag like that?" This is not a question I ever admitted asking, though I'm sure it was on my lips as I stared down at my mother's stretched-out form, studying her body. Years later my mother, still walking through the apartment with a towel tied around her waist, would tell that story laughing, as proof of what she had to endure from her hostile daughter, but also with the confidence of a woman proud of her breasts. If I ever grew breasts, what—or whose—would they be like? Both grandmothers were all bosom; their breasts filled their entire chest (a C at least, if not a D). My mother edged up to a B. My sister and I barely made it to an A. Where did the breasts go? The alphabet in reverse in three generations.

Sometimes it seems as if there is only one body: hers unchanging from age twenty-eight—when she is my new mother—to sixty-eight when she began to die. Her hair went from black (blue black she liked to say) to silver, but the body kept its form and style. How can that be? When I looked at my mother's body, I didn't so much see my future as her irreducible mystery: Why, since she didn't seem to want us, did she have us?

Steedman argues both for a class-bound maternal economics and for a universal psychological view: "Part of the desire to reproduce oneself as a body, as an entity in the real world, lies in conscious memory of someone approving that body." This is especially where her mother, in conscious memory, fails her again. But she moves on to make the wider point of maternal "coldness towards daughters," which draws its power from its conjunction with the daughters' assessment of "the attitude of the social world towards them." In this moment of a double "exclusion"—always a key word for Steedman—the failure of "self-love," which she places "at the root of the wish for a child," takes its fullest meaning and leads to the refusal to reproduce.

Throughout her memoir, when Steedman seeks to analyze maternal rejection ("If it wasn't for you two," her mother moaned, "I could be off somewhere else"; "Never have children dear, they ruin your life"), she insists on the working-class base of this not-wanted-ness and in turn on its essential difference from a middle-class repertoire of relatedness. But when she looks to working-class autobiographies for confirmation of the power of the social world to confer disapproval, Steedman also acknowledges that daughters' "exile" from maternal attention is recorded in all kinds of literary and autobiographical accounts of mothers and daughters, including fairy tales like "The Little Mermaid" and "The Snow Queen," which are not class bound and are in fact foundational to her own accounts of childhood fantasies.

When I first read Landscape, I was hungry for this story of a woman proud to not have had children. I desperately wanted to read the story of a woman who didn't want to reproduce herself. I wanted to make sense of the effects of a certain freedom that felt bizarrely both compelled and chosen. Like Steedman, I thought my mother unloving and unloved. Despite all warnings I kept finding commonalities in our experience that seemed to erase class difference or at least cross class lines. After all, I too could say that my mother's longing shaped my childhood. Asked what she meant by my mother's "ambition," my aunt (her sister, whom I interviewed about our family) said succinctly: "She always wanted a lot more than she had." And there's also a way in which the poor, undereducated immigrants of my grandparents' era shared a need for a narrative of escape of the sort Steedman describes. Growing up, I felt a legacy of deprivation, produced by immigration, and then revived with the Great Depression. Our home life was laced with a deadly anxiety about money and things (I was once beaten for losing the keys to the house, "think what it would cost to replace the locks"); the silent dread that there would never be enough; the manipulations performed to short-circuit desire ("you don't really want . . .").

Most of all, I wanted to say: You don't know what I would have been doing a hundred years ago. Less than a hundred years ago, my grandfather was cutting the cloth your grandmother wove.

"Women mother." This is the first sentence of one of the most influential books of feminist theory to come out of the 1970s, Nancy Chodorow's *The Reproduction of Mothering*. "Women come to want and need primary relationships to children," Chodorow concludes in the last chapter of her book, but in the afterword she admits that her account is "too unqualified," and she modifies her position on a universal desire. "In fact all women do not mother or want to mother," and all women are not "maternal" or "nurturant." (This is Steedman's point but she faults Chodorow for not making more of it.) Chodorow, Steedman objects, is "well aware of the limitations of her account, and knows that it is class and culture bound. Were it not so bound, then the darker social side of the primary relationship between mothers and daughters . . . would have to emerge." For Steedman the breakdown of maternal care, "the removal of the looking-glass," depends exclusively on material deprivation. And yet clearly there are other styles of maternal resentment. There's something about the position of the mother as a social being that seems intolerable, whatever a daughter's class position.

Is there one mother women don't want to become?

This mother is the mother we think didn't love us, the mother we don't think we loved. This is the mother who betrayed us, for whom one daughter should have been enough. This is the mother whose recognition we seek ceaselessly, uselessly, and whose darkness has migrated within us. This is the mother who keeps us imagining— and longing for—the Good Mother.

If your mother didn't love you or didn't show it, what about a father who failed to occupy the place of symbolic power and social authority, which in classic models of the psyche is rightfully his? Taking her distance from feminist theorists who believe in the unqualified power of the mother/daughter bond in the creation of feminine personality, Steedman insists on the crucial difference it makes to a little girl to have a father who wasn't, as she puts it, "a patriarch." Having a father who didn't count, even when he was there.

> His not mattering has an effect like this: I don't quite believe in male power; somehow the iron of patriarchy didn't enter my soul. I accept the idea of male power intellectually, of course (and I will eat my words the day I am raped, or the knife is slipped between my ribs; though I know that will not be the case: in the dreams it is a woman who holds the knife, and only a woman can kill).

Fathers. Mothers. Knives. Who is the woman holding the knife, her mother or herself?

After her father's death, Steedman imagines she can see her father—the way her father was—in the body of other men of his generation walking in the city streets. But she can't *see* her mother. Her mother lives in her dreams. But who is her mother? "She, myself, walks my dreams." You can't see your mother if your mother is yourself.

"You're so cold and thoughtless, you'll die alone and without friends, like Grandma Kipnis" was my mother's refrain whenever she wanted to wound me (I prided myself on my friends) or simply to get my adolescent attention.

In the dream my mother offers me her cold cheek: "Kiss me again," she says, unsmiling but with feeling. Eagle-eye, I was called, because though nearsighted, I never missed a defect in the things she made for me: a seam, a hem, a buttonhole, the fall of a lining. Who trained me to see defects? Shopping, she would get a discount for buying a shirt with a loose button, a stain, a torn hem, all things she could then fix.

I comb the racks, looking for defects. And I find them.

At the end of the chapter in *Landscape* devoted to her father, "A Thin Man," Steedman comments on the fact that after his death she was left with nothing but the knowledge of her illegitimacy. This newly revealed fact comes to confirm the sense of wrongness that

had filled her childhood. He wouldn't, her mother said, give up the
other woman and marry her: "'How could he do it,' she said, 'leave
two nice little girls like you?'" The father might not have mattered,
but however powerless, he nonetheless possessed the crucial power
of patriarchy—to withhold legitimacy.

"He left us without anything, never gave us a thing." This is not
how fairy tales were supposed to turn out. "But daddy, you never
knew me like this. . . . You shouldn't have left us there, you should
have taken me with you. You left me alone; you never laid a hand on
me: the iron didn't enter the soul. You never gave me anything: the
lineaments of an unused freedom." The sadness is accentuated by
the direct address, the only instance in the memoir. But daddy. Two
languages to tell one story. The language of a child's loss ("the iron
didn't enter the soul" is a verse from the *Book of Common Prayer*).
The language of an intellectual's theory. In the intersection of the
two versions lives a daughter with an ambitious wish: the daughter
of neither, the daughter of both.

Like Adrienne Rich, Steedman outlines a narrative of escape: how
to read your way out of stories that don't have you in them or have
you in the wrong part. What do you want to be when you grow up
if you can't see—or can only see to hate—what you might grow up
to be?

"You're so unfeeling, Kay." (Kay, Steedman explains, is the name
she was called at home, one of her father's names.) In "The Snow
Queen," the little boy Kay suffers from having a lump of ice in his
heart. He remains frozen inside until little Gerda finds him and her
hot tears melt him. If you think you have a lump of ice in your heart,
and no one comes to melt it, you grow up frozen. You can wait a
long time for the right tears. The accusation of coldness rings true
because it confirms the anxiety of the fairy tale. What if Kay were
like that coldhearted little boy (her namesake), made cold by the
cruel Snow Queen? Was it really his fault that a piece of ice lodged
in his eye and made him see everything distorted, that another piece
lodged in his heart and he became a child of stone?

In the dreams it is a woman who holds the knife. Who is the
woman wielding the knife, if not Mom? As a seven-year-old reader

of fairy tales, Steedman imagines her parents sitting naked, cutting each other, "making thin surface wounds like lines drawn with a sharp red pencil, from which the blood poured." And the child insists, "She was the most cut, but I knew it was she who did the cutting. I couldn't always see the knife in my father's hand." Despite the contradictory "evidence" of the fantasy, the daughter maintains her belief in the murderous power of the mother she claims to eulogize: "Death of a Good Woman." The fantasy, she remarks later, is a way she had as a child of registering the cost of nourishment the little girls—no longer nursing babies—were made to feel they had generated: "the thin wounds across her breasts pouring forth blood, not milk."

What about the knife in her father's hand? Why is it so much easier to forgive his cuts? He cut his losses. Split the difference. Split and didn't leave. But daddy. A book of retaliation. In *Past Tenses* Steedman admits that *Landscape* is a book "designed to hurt." It is "ungrateful and resentful towards feminism as well." This resentment shows up, she says, in "the pitching of class against gender," in letting class win, "as the more interesting, important, and revelatory interpretive device." And part of letting gender lose entails blaming her mother, all the while attempting to make sense of her mother's life and justifying it in material terms—as a historian.

Steedman explains that she came to write *Landscape for a Good Woman* through another daughter's book, a first-person narrative by Kathleen Woodward called *Jipping Street*, which has at its heart "a working-class mother whose love towards her children was terrible and ambivalent: a mother who was a central and impossible contradiction in her daughter's life." *Jipping Street* gave Steedman permission to render the crux at the heart of her own life: "a relationship . . . between mother and daughter that resulted not in the daughter's wish for a child, but in the daughter's refusal to reproduce herself." In the wake of her mother's death and in response to *Jipping Street*, Steedman writes the embryonic version of *Landscape* that appears in *Truth, Dare or Promise*. In the book most of this material becomes the chapter called "The Weaver's Daughter," which tells her mother's history. The early version of their story begins with a dream and ends with the visit to her mother with which the longer work also ends. It's a dream about women wanting things, wanting in this case a New Look coat: "When I was three, before my sister was born, I had a dream." In the dream, Steedman is a little girl watching a woman dressed in a New Look coat, who is shaking her finger and confusing her about what she wants. Steedman bases her interpretation of this dream—that the woman in the New Look coat was the other woman, the other mother of a little girl whose existence made her family illegitimate—on the dress she herself is wearing, the dress of the three-year-old in the snapshot with her mother. The reconstruction of this dream provides the structure of the memoir, the memory of her mother complaining that she and her sister were "two living barriers to twenty yards of cloth." It's only later that she learns the name of the coat's fabric: gabardine. The language of my own childhood returns: gabardine, serge, melton. The fabrics of identity. Tailored mysteries.

My mother's father wanted to put the shtetl behind him. He believed in the education plot, the Jewish immigrant rise through the next generation: four children—the boys, a lawyer and a doctor; the girls, schoolteachers. Grandpa, my aunt explains, was ambitious. "Chamber music at home. Ballet lessons. All paid for out of the tailor's shop one flight up on West Thirty-fifth Street. When these adult children were starting their own families in the late 1930s and early '40s, Grandpa rented a large house on the Jersey shore. The three married but impecunious offspring summer together in rented splendor, subsidized by the earnings of the bachelor doctor son. The women look after their new babies, the men commute to the city. My father is a fledgling lawyer, operating on promise; my parents barely pay the rent. My mother works for my uncle the doctor to make ends meet. She has a black maid at home who cleans, cooks, and looks after me, but she also returns bottles to the grocery store for the deposit, sews her own clothes and shops for bargains on Fourteenth Street. I wear handmade pinafores, and later coats made by my grandfather.

Home movies. The summer of 1941. The camera pans over beds of red tulips that border a huge white Victorian house. On the lawn of luxury, I receive, according to the handwriting on the yellow Kodak box, a manicure from my mother. I am six months old. Uncle Dave (aka Dr. Miller) drives up in his convertible, with the top down. He opens his doctor's bag. Say ah.

The summer of 1942. I'm a toddler with creases in my thighs. I'm the only girl, with three boy cousins. My uncle rubs me against his face, waltzes me in the sun. My grandparents fondle me. I am passed from one set of arms to another. I look into the camera—my father's gaze—and I smile, trustingly. I splash around in the water and pretend to swim. It's Technicolor, my skin is the color of melba toast, my eyes are green, and, amazingly, I'm blond.

The summer of 1944. My sister, Ronna, and my cousin Carol have entered the scene. My hair has turned brown. Paradise is lost. Have I spent my entire life trying to retrieve that moment—the face of a little girl whose father and mother loved her? The home movies star me but they also star Mommy and feature my little sister, the "gushy baby," I called her, as I kneaded her delectable flesh. It's my life, yes, but I'm not alone. We're all in this together.

"For we think back through our mothers if we are women." That sentence from Virginia Woolf's feminist classic *A Room of One's Own* has been cited over and over in discussions of women's writing. These memoirs make that metaphorical notion of women's literary history strikingly literal—when a woman writes her life through a dream of her mother's frustrated desire. What happens to your own longing when it is passed through the mesh of a mother's wish that, at least some of the time, you didn't exist? The mother's disappointment, the naked want, the longings unsatisfied, become a daughter's legacy. The legacy of *Jipping Street* is complex. "What was given, perhaps, was an area of freedom: an acknowledgement that it is *all right* not to love your mother, and that mothers may often not love you."

We read for what we need to find.

Both Steedman and Rich recount a palpable shift away from the mother's body and date it with the birth of their little sister: "I don't remember," Rich writes in *Of Woman Born*, "when it was that my mother's feminine sensuousness, the reality of her body, began to give way for me to the charisma of my father's assertive mind and temperament; perhaps when my sister was just born, and he began teaching me to read." In both cases we're dealing, as Steedman puts it in a parenthetical (Freudian) aside, with "an old, conventional story, every eldest daughter's tale."

"When I was three before my sister was born." These are the words that introduce the dream out of which *Landscape* emerges; it is also the caption of the snapshot of a blond girl with a huge head of fuzzy hair sitting on a lawn in summer next to her mother. Her mother is wearing a summer frock and a broad-brimmed straw hat. She has a newspaper spread out on her lap; the little girl, a doll. It's a picnic in 1950. At this level of detail (the photo is pretty much of a blur), class assignment is indecipherable. The scene is urban pastoral. There are no knives in sight.

Before her sister was born. Before the expulsion from Eden that came with her sister's birth.

Watching home movies was always, my mother used to complain, "such a production." Unearthing the ancient projector buried at the back of the closet, finding the screen, threading the film. By the time I remember watching the movies, it was already the fifties. The glamour of the forties had passed; my parents were no longer sleekly fashionable; they had entered bicker mode and I had long since ceased being adorable. Watching these movies with my parents was no different from any other regular episode of family war. The contrast between our cramped daily reality and the obvious charm of the already mythical past made the showings excruciating exercises in nuclear depression. The film would jam or break. My mother would then yell at my father, the famous withering single syllable—"Lou"— which here meant not only the specific problem (the projector), but the generic assault. "Why can't you get anything right?" Big white dots would explode on the screen indicating that the movie was over; my sister and I would run to the bathroom. Since each film lasted only a few minutes, and there was no way to freeze the frame, each moment was a flash, a glimpse of a past already not remembered. ("Don't you remember the dollhouse Grandpa built for you, the swing?") No matter how I longed for my little princess past, I could not bring back the feeling of what it was to be blond, to be at the center of love.

Expulsion from Eden is not the only way for a daughter to understand the terms of her childhood. The sense of loss that haunts these little girls is countered vividly by Annie Ernaux's knowledge of belonging to a place that however constraining allows her to leave and then to return in memory with a forgiving eye. In *A Woman's Story* Ernaux re-creates a small child's fascinated view of her mother's body: "When she put on lipstick, she always started with the heart-shaped bit in the middle. She turned to face the wall when she fastened her corset. Her flesh bulged through the criss-cross of laces, joined together at her waist by a knot and a small rosette. I knew every detail of her body. I though that I would grow up to become her." For Ernaux, this promise is a source of intense pleasure: "I am sitting on the crossbar of my father's bike, while she rides down the slope ahead of us, her back straight, the seat firmly wedged between her buttocks. . . . I believe we were both in love with my mother."

I thought that I would grow up to become her. This prospect is desired as much as it is dreaded.

In powerful contrast to Steedman's painful struggle to be free of her mother, all the while demonstrating her connection to her, Ernaux's memoir is shaped by the lure of what I'm tempted to call "matrophilia," the loving desire to become one's mother. (This pull to resemblance is what Hope Edelman calls in *Motherless Daughters* "matridentity." The logic of "matridentity" repeats that of matrophobia, "its twin sister," and goes like this: "Aren't my mother and I really, underneath it all, exactly the same?") Despite or even through the displacement and rupture a university education produces, Ernaux returns in loving memory to her mother's body, to the seduction of union. "Throughout the ten months I was writing this book," Ernaux reveals toward the end of her memoir, "I dreamed of her almost every night. Once I was lying in the middle of a stream, caught between two currents. From my genitals, smooth again like a young girl's, from between my thighs, long tapering plants floated limply. The body they came from was not only mine, it was also my mother's." *A Woman's Story* (in French *Une femme*) is an act of emotional reconnection that passes through two bodies joined in resemblance. One woman. But the book depends on their separateness: "I believe I am writing about my mother because it is my turn to bring her into the world." Two lives separated by one book.

The body they came from was not only mine, it was also my mother's.

Ernaux interweaves the trajectory of their two lives in a double and overlapping chronology: her mother's movement out of the peasantry into the life of small shopkeepers; her own, fostered by her mother, out of that world into a bourgeois professional class. The end of the mother's life is shaped by the nightmare effects of Alzheimer's disease, the daughter's midlife entails a coming to terms with that illness and the death of both parents.

A Woman's Story locates the fault lines in the mother/daughter territory in the familial dramas of adolescence, always a central moment in autobiography. Adolescence represents a turning point in self-definition, and children start wanting a story of their own making. Classically, the adolescent moment for daughters has been a conflict between women over sexual autonomy, a violence located around the body. Here the tension explodes in outbursts of rage over clothes: "'You're not going out like *that*?'" "We both knew," Ernaux writes, "what to expect from each other: she knew I longed to seduce the boys, I knew she was terrified I would 'have an accident,' in other words, that I would start to sleep around and get pregnant." The daughter's evaluation of this struggle takes the succinct form of a remembered guilty wish: "Sometimes I imagined her death would have meant nothing to me."

"Why did my mother's death shake me so deeply?"

Violence and reparation. Writing within the year immediately after her mother's death, Ernaux talks about the difficulty of getting her mother straight: "To get away from these oscillating views, which come from my earliest childhood, I try to describe and explain her life as if I were writing about someone else's mother and a daughter who wasn't me." But this displacement designed to create objectivity is pierced by the effects of memory: "Still, though I try to write as neutrally as possible, certain expressions, such as 'if you ever have an accident . . . ,' can never be neutral for me, while others, for instance, 'the denial of one's own body and sexuality,' remain totally abstract. When I remember these expressions," Ernaux concludes surprisingly, "I experience the same feeling of depression I had when I was sixteen, and fleetingly, I confuse the woman who influenced me most with an African mother pinning her daughter's arms behind her back while the village midwife slices off the girl's clitoris." While the reference to clitoridectomy is a relative commonplace in certain kinds of feminist discourse, it's quite startling in this writerly rememoration. Ernaux, whose mother's fear that her daughter's pregnancy would keep her from a bright and open future, seems to conjure the maternal assault as a local not global intervention—the cruelty of maternal complicity in circumscribing women's desire. "The denial of one's own body and sexuality." The frozen but fighting words of feminist revolt uttered in struggle. The mother worries about social freedom for her daughter, bought at the price of parental sacrifice. But the daughter's pleasure becomes hostage to the mother's fear. "If you ever have an accident." In these excruciating moments of adolescent unfreedom, a mother's power makes its way into the recesses of sexual need. The stories are at odds with each other. Look at all we have done for you. Now you want to throw it all away.

Ernaux's rage against her mother is located in the body, the body that ties her to class: "I was ashamed of her brusque manners and speech, especially when I realized how alike we were. I blamed her for being someone who I, by moving into new circles, no longer wanted to be. I discovered that there was a world of difference between wanting to be educated and actually acquiring that knowledge." The child moves into another world by virtue of an experience the less-educated parent has wanted the child to have, without wanting the child to change. When Annie leaves home for further schooling, her departure is marked by a summary of the mother's view of their relation in social terms: "Sometimes she saw her own daughter as a class enemy."

"If you ever have an accident" is the mother's language for the possibility of a double betrayal woven of sex and class. The daughter's pleasure becomes the mother's anxiety about reproduction, which in turn codes an anxiety about class identity. In *A Man's Place*, the earlier memoir about her father, Ernaux insists on the importance for her parents of controlling their class future. "He had learned the essential condition for not reproducing the misery of the previous generation: not to forget oneself in a woman. (Ernaux's parents determine not to reproduce their parent's poverty by having only one child; when their first and only child dies, they replace her with Annie.) The mother fears that the daughter's adolescent rebellion, with its bourgeois overtones of scorn for social convention, will subvert the education plot she has subscribed to, out of the working class into middle-class comfort. She demands loyalty—recognition by the daughter of her values, authority, and vision—but resigns herself to disappointment and betrayal.

Looking sexy. I never had the body for the part. But in those days sexy was more a message than a figure (maybe that's how I consoled myself). We looked—we hoped—like beatniks, or at least Bohemians: as though we lived not, for instance, on the Upper West Side but downtown in the Village. The goal in New York in the late fifties, as Rachel Brownstein named it in Becoming a Heroine, *was studied anonymity: "black turtleneck, black skirt, black stockings, black shoes, and a black coat, occasionally enlivened by something grey." I preferred—beneath my black hair and black turtleneck—jeans and dirty, torn sneakers. My mother usually got stuck on the dirty, torn sneakers. But if the look wasn't sexy, it was meant as a rebuke and an invitation. It said, I don't want to be a virgin. This my father understood. If you go to a boy's apartment, he would thunder— when I was forced to confess my plans for the evening—who will believe you when you testify in the paternity suit? I was always impressed by the leap from the outfit to the jury box; my father was not only a lawyer—he was a self-appointed judge. When I started receiving obscene phone calls, my mother triumphed: News of my "reputation" had spread. Why bother, then, to tell them that—technically at least—I still was a virgin.*

.   .   .

"Until I married, I still belonged to her, even when we were living apart." Leaving the mother behind, Ernaux also fears the inexorability of class betrayal, precisely through an education that gives her access to new language, new powers of interpretation, and new models of self-conscious behavior. The last third of the memoir, which is marked by the death of Ernaux's father, recounts the attempt of the two women to live together in the daughter's house. The experiment of their life together reveals the complicated ways in which class alignments can shift within a family over the time of its own history. At her daughter's house, the mother feels out of place: "I don't think I belong here." This is not cast, as it might be in an American context, as a psychological problem. For Ernaux it's a social dilemma in which her mother looks for work to do in the house to help out, in order, she says jokingly, to pay her way. "It took me a long time to realize," Ernaux writes, "that the feeling of unease my mother experienced in my own house was no different from what I had felt as a teenager when I was introduced to people a 'cut above us.'" She analyzes the differences that now separate them, despite her continued identification with her mother's body and desires. "I also realized that in pretending to act like the hired help, she instinctively translated the real cultural domination of her children's reading *Le Monde* or listening to Bach into an imaginary economic domination of boss over worker: her form of revolt." Social distinctions came to infect the mother/daughter relation within the family and under the same roof. The story of what those differences finally mean is inseparable in Ernaux's narrative from the memoir project itself. To memorialize her mother is to map the passage between their two worlds, keeping both alive. It is in this double vision that Ernaux's view of class assignments, and their power to shape one's relation to the world, differs from Steedman's.

In a letter she wrote to me in response to seeing an earlier form of this chapter, Ernaux declared in unambiguous terms her solidarity with Steedman's sense of exclusion from the world of her readers—especially her women readers. She emphasized her sense of marginality, of belonging to a place on the map of social life undreamt of in the unself-consciousness of the middle class. "I am persuaded," she went on to say, "that social origins structure the individual first and that gender comes after." But where Ernaux differs from Steedman has specifically to do with what she calls the narrator's "present situation." Composing the story of her life, Ernaux said, she "passed into 'the other world.'" The place she writes from she defines as "an in-between"—a place between the two worlds. "Through the work of memory, the origin of my vision of the world," she explained, "I belong to the dominated world; by intellectual tools, culture, daily life to the dominant world. That could also be called having no place." The memoirist's material is necessarily engaged in a negotiation between these two places, whether or not they are plotted out in class terms. The world of childhood, of the person we were before, the person who survives within us in memory, is forever the site to which the writer returns in her mind. At the same time, the childhood scene, transformed by time and space, cannot help but pass through the sieve of composition only to emerge already different from what it was. Having "no place" is a way of always having two places at once, in two times. The origins are caught, snagged in the net of their writing.

Steedman's attempt to separate from her mother displays an almost ontological resentment, which is radically unlike Ernaux's essentially adolescent rites of passage that end when she becomes an adult. She recalls a letter to a friend during vacation from the university in which she describes spending the evening with her mother, "refusing to go out, holding tight to my guilt and duty, knowing that I *was* her, and that I must keep her company." Despite this overidentification, which seems to freeze the daughter into immobility, like Ernaux, Steedman has in fact moved on: She has become a social historian. The University of Sussex, where she was a student in 1965, is another vantage point from which she can view her mother's story, even if the cultural narratives available to the women of her generation and class do not feature their scenarios. "And should I have met a woman like me (there must have been some . . .) we could not have talked of escape except within a literary framework . . . ignorant of the material stepping-stones of our escape: clothes, shoes, make-up." *Landscape* sets itself the task of producing that literary framework, supplying that missing text through the auto/biography of two working-class women.

When she speaks about her years at the university, Steedman alludes to the effects of the process she names as "embourgeoisement and state education"—what Ernaux calls her passage into the "dominant world." Steedman acknowledges the fact of this passage through her professional identity as a historian. Beyond that, as readers we come up against a silence which has everything to do with the elusive quality of her narrative. We are left in the dark about the ways in which Steedman's childhood stories continue to be lived in the writing present. Blanks of discretion white out the adult story of conflict and desire.

For instance, when Steedman goes to visit her dying mother, this is the first time, we learn, that they have seen each other in *nine years* (except, she specifies later in passing, at her father's funeral). This break is not explained. We are left to conjecture about what's happened, though Steedman alludes to the separation obliquely. Her father, she writes, "was genuinely shocked when, at twenty-seven, I wrote to my mother and said that I didn't want to see her for a while because she upset me so much." We are left to speculate about why, after years of feeling so fiercely attached to her mother—thinking she *was* her—she deliberately broke the connection.

In the late seventies, my sister, who at the beginning of the sixties had set out to declass herself through her relations and activities and to separate herself from our middle-class parents, decided to quit her job as a day-care worker and try to earn her living as a potter. What stood between this desire and her ability to put it into practice was the price of a kiln, a basic element of a potter's studio. My mother offered to pay for the equipment, and by the way, she thought, of encouragement, added jokingly: "Don't worry, if it doesn't work out I can take it as a business loss on my taxes." A few days later, she received a note from my sister in which she announced that in view of our mother's lack of confidence in her ability to make a go of it—she always "rained on her parade"—she would not be seeing her for a while. And she didn't. Almost five years later my sister reluctantly came to see our mother who was rapidly dying of cancer. Our mother betrayed neither anger nor surprise when her daughter showed up, but the wounds remained open on both sides. My sister wrote my mother out of her life. My mother wrote my sister out of her will.

In *Truth, Dare or Promise*, Steedman offers a partial explanation for the space she puts between her mother and herself. It has to do with not living up to what she took to be her mother's expectations. Steedman describes what it was like to be at the university and have her thesis rejected; what it was like to go on—with a sense of defeat—to be an elementary school teacher for eight difficult years. "One reason I didn't see my mother during that time," she speculates, "is that I knew what she thought: was it all for this? A teacher—like being a nurse or a policeman, something I could have done anyway, without her sacrifice. For the first time, I'd let her down." These autobiographical reflections give voice to what in the memoir remains unstated: the complicity between mother and daughter, their shared stake in the education and profession: "I was—and am—the first person in my family ever to have stayed at school beyond the compulsory leaving age."

Was it all for this? Steedman thinks she knows what her mother thinks because she thinks she is her mother. She doesn't want to see her own sense of failure mirrored in her mother's face, the face of the woman who holds the knife. (Of course if you are your mother, you turn the knife on yourself.) Like little children who cover their eyes and think you can't see them, if you don't go and see your mother, she can't see you. But you see you. In an essay called "Perversion," Adam Phillips remarks on the degree to which we overvalue the disappointment we experience and cause: "Mothers, in fact, do not let their children down, even though both mothers and children are keen to see it this way: they simply lead their lives." Perhaps this should be reversed: Children, in fact, do not let their mothers down, they simply lead their lives. But we children seem to need to feel this disappointment. Our own disappointment in ourselves would be too much to bear. We continue to see ourselves, even if we practice the hide-and-seek of not telling at the heart of any autobiographical project.

In the memoir itself, however, Steedman refuses to supply a motive for the nine-year separation, and she says only this about their final meeting: "An hour later I came away believing that I admired a woman who could, in these circumstances and in some pain, treat me as if I had just stepped round the corner for a packet of tea." This was, Steedman remarks in a tone that is eerily jubilant, the way things had always been: "We were truly illegitimate, outside any law of recognition: the mirror broken, a lump of ice for a heart." Without the mirroring of maternal approval that leads the daughter to want to reproduce, the bond between mother and daughter seems permanently damaged, ruptured beyond repair. Or perhaps it's the other way round. Perhaps we should interpret the daughter's admiration for her mother's indifference as confirmation of their ultimate bond: the mother in myself. In the early twenty-page version of her memoir, Steedman includes an explanatory remark about this moment that she subsequently deletes: "Talking to my sister on the phone about the visit she insisted that the feeling of being absent in my mother's presence was nothing to do with the illness, was the emotional underpinning of our childhood." And the sentence above ends differently in Steedman's short narrative: "We were truly *illegitimate*, our selves *not there*." If to be in the mother's presence is to not exist or to exist in unbearable loneliness, installing absence at the center of the relation would indeed seem the key to survival. I can be there only if she isn't there. So I won't go back. My self not there.

It's the night before a big talk. I'm going to address an audience of hundreds of women, feminists who have come to a conference at Barnard College. (I'm an assistant professor of French across the street at Columbia.) I've never spoken before such a large group, and I'm sick with fear. I've been asked to speak personally, which I've never done in public. I'm going to describe my room—how I live in it alone and try to write. I'm in my late thirties, not married, and in love with a married man (that's not part of the talk); more than anything I value my work. It's 1978, I'm an untenured assistant professor, and there are no tenure-track jobs in French on the horizon.

My mother and I talk on the phone. She is buoyant, garrulous. She has called because there's a story she wants to tell me. "It's hilarious," she says. She was standing on a subway platform waiting for a train and found herself witness to a conversation between my lover (don't ask why I've told my mother about him), who is in his early fifties, and a young woman. The woman was looking up at him with admiration, he was basking in it. As I listen to my mother, jealousy joins the panic and I begin to sink. I'm still waiting, dry-mouthed, for the hilarious part. My heart is paying attention, though my mind is gone. Racing. It must have been a student. He couldn't possibly be having an affair in addition to ours. "Wasn't it a coincidence," she says, "that we should have been on the same platform. He really is quite a ladies' man, you know." "He's Italian," I say defensively. "They always flirt. It doesn't mean anything. It must have been one of his students." "I thought you would be amused," she concludes.

How and where would I begin trying to make her understand that she's just taken my breath away? I am hopelessly in love with a man for whom I am an episode. We are not going to run away together; he will not, as the expression goes, leave his wife for me, give up his children, who are little. How can my mother not know that despite my theories of liberation, I live abjectly for our time together, crave his embrace, make his touch the center of my world. How can she know, not know this and think, think I would be amused. "Ma, it's the night before my talk." And I don't say any of this to her. Because I know she would reply from her own rage as injured mother: "How can you think I would say something to hurt you?" And then I would have to explain again about the unconscious. And then her voice would harden, since to invoke her unconscious is to blame her. My mother, after all, is the one who, when I began therapy, insisted on her right to see the therapist in order to tell him what really had happened in my childhood, and why I was wrong.

What are we looking to get from these women who don't know we are there? We keep hoping they will learn, hoping we will get through, hoping even that we will learn. This is a story that attracts clichés. My sister didn't want my mother to "rain on her parade." I went back, knowing that each time my mother would "burst my bubble." And yet the mothers keep taking us back and coming after us for more, too. "Children," Françoise de Beauvoir, a mother who passed on the unhappiness of her childhood to her daughters, complained, "don't always understand their parents." But this misses the point. A parent's failure to recognize a child's reality—to respect its fragility—enacts a violence that can never be reciprocal, even if it seems to get paid back.

There is a dark passion in daughters to get credit (even a consolation prize) for inventing a new way of being in the world, at least for trying. It's hard to know what you have to show in order to get credit (A for effort) when you have not been successful in conventional terms. And especially when the terms in which you measure your progress in self-invention are not your mother's, neither what she desired for herself, nor for you. A New Look coat. A house. Worldly success. Marriage. A child. Or none of the above. Something that has no name and no object. There's a peculiar violence between mother and daughter that comes from the coexistence of repudiation (I'm nothing like you) and overidentification (I thought I *was* you). We don't choose our mothers any more than they choose us. And we only tell their story through ourselves. "It is hard," Rich admits in *Of Woman Born*, "to write about my own mother. Whatever I do write, it is my story I am telling, my version of the past. If she were to tell her own story other landscapes would be revealed. But in my landscape or hers, there would be old, smoldering patches of deep-burning anger." Why so much anger in the landscape?

In her memoir *Taking It like a Woman* (one of the autobiographies Steedman said she felt excluded from) British sociologist Ann Oakley writes: "Voices rise and fall but mostly rise. Everyone is tired, everyone has needs. Robin [her husband] has a look of harassed discontent about him, as though he did not really choose this when he chose to 'have' a family. Neither did I—or they, for that matter. We all would like peace and an army of slaves. What we get is noise and fragmented attention." What does it mean to reproduce? "I am a member of this second nuclear family," Oakley writes, "as I was a member of my first for powerful historical reasons. Coming from one, I felt impelled to create another. I cannot wipe out that particular historical pattern: all we can do is make this second family different from the first." What's at stake more broadly, I think, is understanding, at the end of the twentieth century, the nature of that compulsion as a production and a construction. As Judith Butler writes (rereading *The Second Sex*): "If motherhood becomes a choice, then what else is possible?"

It's 1981, three years after my talk at Barnard. I've just gotten tenure there and I'm running the Women's Studies Program. There's to be a panel celebrating the tenth anniversary of the Women's Center. I'm going to speak as the director of the program. I have not mentioned this to my mother. I still feel about my mother coming to see me perform just as I did in my junior high on Open School Day, when I feigned laryngitis (she was not deceived) in order not to read my paper in front of her. But since that Barnard conference three years ago, she's been on the center's mailing list. "Why didn't you tell me you were going to speak?" "I didn't think you would be interested." "Why did you think I wouldn't be interested? You know I'm interested in what you do." "Well, you're not a feminist." "Maybe I'm not a feminist the way you're a feminist but that doesn't mean I'm not a feminist. I believe in women's rights." (Silent groan.) Rather than repeat my analysis of how you can't be a feminist if your husband supports you, even if you have worked part-time, I try more junior high: "Well, you can come if you want to, but I'm going to be very busy and won't be able to talk to you. You'll have to have lunch by yourself, I'll be at a table with the speakers." She says she's coming anyway.

My mother comes early to see my new office, which I share with a student assistant, who works for the program six hours a week; a hole in the wall behind the commons in which the event is to be held, but my first office to myself. She doesn't really want to see the office, she wants to show me a button she's found to replace the one on I've lost on my pea coat (she's bought us the same jacket in different colors). She's pleased with herself and eager to detail the trouble she's gone to in order for me to exclaim what a great find it is, what a bargain, and how nice it was of her to do this for me. After all, she's busy too. Fine, it's fine, but I don't want to think about buttons now, I have to give a talk. I shove her into the hall, make her go find a seat by herself.

I am forty years old. She is sixty-eight. She is still fixing my clothes, finding buttons, shortening hems, letting out and taking in waists. A tailor's daughter, whose Hebrew name (Malka), she used to say, means queen. I am still ungratefully accepting her services. She is dying but we don't know it. If we knew it, we would still have the fight.

There seems to be a particular rage both *in* and *between* mothers and daughters that comes from women's inability to *choose* motherhood, in the sense that they cannot possibly know *what* they are choosing. (Coming from one, I feel impelled to create another. The possibility of motherhood is always too close to home to be a choice.) And of course, in not choosing it, to know *what* has been refused. These are the stories still untold. Whether or not a daughter becomes a mother, whether or not this is an accident of fate or an existential choice, the re-creation of the mother in writing after her death can be a way of coming to terms with the power of that unchosen bond between women.

The memoir of the other, the dead mother, is both for oneself and for others. For Ernaux, this re-creation has the effect of giving her private mother her public due: "Over the past few days," Ernaux explains in the writing notes that guide the reading of the memoir, "I have found it more and more difficult to write, possibly because I would like never to reach this point. And yet I know I shall have no peace of mind until I find the words which will unite the demented woman she had become with the strong, radiant woman she once was." When her mother starts talking to imaginary people, Ernaux first puts her hands over her ears not to hear. Then, "to make the thought bearable," she describes what's happening on a scrap of paper: "Maman's talking to herself." Finally, she explains toward the memoir's close, "I'm writing those same words now, but for other people, so that they can understand." Perhaps the memoir is not the debt to the parents repaid through caring for one's own children, but a writer's debt for the material itself. The figure of indebtedness that Ernaux assigns herself in this project is that of "archivist." It is to her that falls the task of recording the end of a certain tradition— of "household tips which lessened the strain of poverty," of a certain maternal lore passed on from mother to daughter.

There is another task at hand. By virtue of changing classes, by establishing a link between making a life and writing one, Ernaux transforms the meaning of household tips. Her mother died, Ernaux writes in the memoir's final paragraphs, "eight days before Simone de Beauvoir." She describes her mother's generosity. "She preferred giving to everybody, rather than taking from them." And then asks rhetorically, "Isn't writing also a way of giving." I puzzled over the reference to Beauvoir in these closing moments. In writing to me about this chapter, Ernaux explained that she invoked Beauvoir's death at the end of her book out of what she calls a sense of justice. She wanted, she said, "to connect the image of a woman who had counted intellectually for me with that of a woman, my mother, who, in my unconscious thoughts, resembled her a great deal, by her will to freedom. At the same time, it was a way of saying that born at almost the same period (1908 and 1906), they led lives light years apart. One exceptional, the other like many others, and bringing them together in the text was perhaps a way of reestablishing justice." But this interpretation, she confesses, came to her after the fact, after my question.

Reestablishing justice. For Ernaux, as for Steedman, Beauvoir is a figure who "counted intellectually." Reading *The Second Sex* at eighteen, Ernaux acknowledged, "was a revelation." But *Memoirs of a Dutiful Daughter* (the first volume of Beauvoir's autobiography), Ernaux added, was a book from which she felt excluded because of Beauvoir's blindness to her own class privilege. In the frame to *Landscape*, the two-page prelude entitled "Death of a Good Woman," Steedman focuses on Françoise de Beauvoir's final hours. "Simone de Beauvoir wrote of her mother's death, said that in spite of the pain it was an easy one: an upper-class death. Outside, for the poor, dying is a different matter." But by the exclusive emphasis on class, this account omits the original appearance of the phrase, and with it, the heart of Beauvoir's irony.

Maman had almost lost consciousness. Suddenly she cried, "I can't breathe!" Her mouth opened, her eyes stared wide, huge in that wasted, ravaged face: with a spasm she entered into coma. . . .
Already she was no longer there—her heart was beating and she breathed, sitting there with glassy eyes that saw nothing. And then it

was over. "The doctors said she would go out like a candle: it wasn't like that at all," said my sister, sobbing.

"But, Madame," replied the nurse, "I assure you it was a very easy death."

Beauvoir's commitment to demystifying human experience, to seeing identity as the effect of a construction, compels her to refuse the clichés of death ("there is no such thing as a natural death") just as she famously refused the clichés of life ("one is not born, rather one becomes a woman"). Beauvoir scrupulously charts the tension between the living's caretaking and the dying's suffering: "Without our obstinate watchfulness she would have suffered far more. For indeed, comparatively speaking, her death was an easy one." But to make the comparison does not erase the death work of the body as a "defenseless thing," which gives Beauvoir, we might say, her material. The memoir graphs this body in pain, a body located and even rooted in class distinctions. Yet in the end, what we retain is less the fact that class markers divide bodies—the screen that blocks the gaze of the dying poor—than the fact that bodies demand our attention. Despite the announced transparency of the "curtainless bedroom" in which Steedman declares that the origins of her story are to be located, is not class also the screen, the "good mother" screen, that stands between a daughter and the rage of longing at work in her own project?

The images of Ernaux's mother "confused" with the African mother participating in her daughter's clitoridectomy and of Steedman's mother as the dream woman with the knife suggest something important about the acts of separation through which a daughter leaves home to become a writer, a writer who returns in memory to tell that story. I think we should see the threatened knife cut not only as a metaphor for the mother's resistance to the daughter's wish for autonomy but for the daughter's rage to be free of maternal power—her need to leave the mother behind. The fear of separation, these books imply, is mutual, and these images are its signature. This is not to say that separation is always fatal (Ernaux seeks to maintain connection to her past, however difficult the return trip proves to be). Steedman describes the feeling of bondage in the very terms of matrophobia that Rich defined: "I was to end up ten, indeed twenty years later, believing that my identification was entirely with her, that whilst hating her, I was her; and there was no escape." For Steedman, it seems, it was only by rupturing the bonds that tied mother and daughter so tightly to each other that she could move out of the maternal orbit and into the writer's space. By making herself into a case study, however, we might argue that she did reproduce herself, especially if we understand the "autobiographical desire par excellence," critic Barbara Johnson suggests in "My Monster/My Self" as "the desire for resemblance, the desire to create a being like oneself." Someone like one's mother.

For years, whenever I was depressed, my mother would recommend exercise (she also was big on cold showers). "Why don't you get out and do something," she would say impatiently. But I would refuse to move, except for dancing and sex. I couldn't see what all that exercise did for her. It was boring, and talking about it more boring still—especially tennis, life as a tennis game, metaphors of losing and winning, ugh. When I stopped smoking (I had decided that I would stop if I got tenure) and gained twelve pounds that I couldn't seem to lose by my usual strategies, I decided to take up running. I started running at forty while my mother was dying of lung cancer—unable to leave the house.

My mother often said that she missed her father, that she thought of him every day. "Grandpa and I would go for walks around the reservoir. He talked to me about everything, his worries about money, how he was going to find the money to send Dave to medical school" (the girls would address envelopes to raise funds for their brother's medical school kitty). When I run around the same reservoir now, still weighing more than I would like to, I think about how much my mother loved her father, about what it would mean to live your life thinking of and loving someone dead. Have I become my mother or just someone like her?

The metaphor of the cut supplies powerful figures for thinking about contemporary autobiographical writing by women, especially when the life narrative entails, as it so often does, telling a mother's story—in her place. Leaving home has always been a condition, often a metaphorical one, for writing an autobiography. For women this departure does not go easily, even at the end of the twentieth century. "And the one doesn't stir," Luce Irigaray wrote, describing the overattachment that painfully immobilizes mothers and daughter, "without the other." The daughter's story reads something like this: You need to separate from your mother. You leave home, cut yourself off (there is always, as we've seen, a cut, a wounding). You write about this. What you left is your material. You make reparation for your leaving by writing, and by this act you return home, only as author, not authored. You've written the story, rewritten the story that wrote you. Earned and betrayed the bequest.

The maternal memoir in which autobiography and biography blur may well be the perfect form for telling that story, since it embodies the irreducible ambiguity of the ties of likeness. Not least of all because your mother isn't yourself. Or is she? "Written autobiography," Steedman remarks in *Past Tenses* about *Landscape*, "has to end in the figure of the writer," which is why, she concludes in a parenthesis, "you have to see that the good woman is me. . . ."

In a British public television program called *Beauvoir's Daughters*, Ann Oakley remarks that for women of her generation (she was born in 1944) Beauvoir was like a mother: "In that way, she's been the Mother, the mother we wished we'd had."

The mother we wished we'd had.

"She died like this. I didn't witness it. My niece told me this." When Steedman says her mother died alone, it means that *she* wasn't there. They missed each other in death as they had in life. My mother died alone means *I* wasn't there. Beauvoir wasn't present at the moment of her mother's easy death. Neither was Ernaux. Perhaps writing about your dead mother is a way of bearing witness to what you didn't see so that you will always remember what you missed.

I was ending my first year as the director of the Women's Studies Program. In April, I was in the dean's office doing business, getting down to cases— we had moved away from his desk and over to the leather couch in order to review the curriculum for the fall semester, playing at being . . . colleagues. I was trying to save "The Invisible Woman," a course about "The Lesbian Literary Tradition" (only the first part of the title appeared on the student transcripts) that the program offered on a regular basis. Regularly, the dean would try to persuade the program not to offer it. We were deep in negotiations, huddled over the budget pages—a struggle I perversely enjoyed and was getting good at—when the call came. The secretary buzzed the dean. I had warned him in my coolest, most professional persona that this might happen ("I'm expecting an important call," I announced, "please have your secretary . . .") but was still startled when it did, just the way it does on TV. Life intrudes on business, takes you by surprise. Takes your breath away. "I have to go," I said, "my mother is dead." I walked down Broadway, down the half mile of city blocks that had separated school from home when I was a student at Barnard myself in the late fifties. Then, walking up to Barnard was a daily attempt to leave home; two decades later, I was still returning. But now my oldest intimate was gone.

Now, I thought, now my real life would begin.

The Miller family, New York, circa 1920.

4

THE ART OF SURVIVAL: MOM, MURDER, MEMORY

Upon my body is superimposed
the map of a Europe I never knew:
my olive skin, my eyes, my hips, my nose
all mark me as an Ashkenazi Jew
if anyone were looking for a mark
to indicate the designated prey.
I'm more the Jew pursued in the dark
than the scrubbed Yank marching through Normandy.

MARILYN HACKER, "August Journal"

An engine, an engine
Chuffing me off like a Jew.
A Jew to Dachau, Auschwitz, Belsen.
I began to talk like a Jew.
I think I may well be a Jew.

SYLVIA PLATH, "Daddy"

A few years ago, I joined a health club called the Paris. Given my history as a Francophile, I might have chosen the club for the name, but its real appeal was the location: a two-block walk from my apartment. Members were entitled to a free orientation session. The trainer assigned to show me around the daunting array of exercise machines aligned in front of the floor-to-ceiling mirrors was named T.W. I would have preferred one of the women trainers, or at least a man not known by his initials, but I didn't seem to have a choice. (Besides, once he had measured my thighs, what else was there to fear?) Midway through my initiation into the world of what the French call musculation, *we arrived at a machine labeled* SHOULDER PRESS. *As I arranged myself on the bench and attempted to raise the bar*

97

over my head at the first level of weights, T.W. explained: "This is for Hadassah arms." Responding to my blank stare, he pointed to my triceps. Hadassah arms. The image conjured by the expression came sharply into focus: the fold of soft flesh that lines the underarm of an aging female body. I saw a large older woman sitting behind a banquet table at a generic Jewish event, wearing a sleeveless dress or maybe a strapless evening gown in a pastel-colored chiffon that set off her jewelry but emphasized the vulnerable cast of her arms. She seemed self-satisfied, even smug, certainly oblivious to the state of her triceps. I suddenly realized that I had identified her look of complacency with a matronly style that I obscurely feared might someday be my own. Despite the fact that physically she was quite different from my own mother (who played tennis and never attended "functions"), the Hadassah lady represented a feminine incarnation I dreaded. Hadassah was a code word that had come to summarize the horrors of the adult female destiny that awaited girls like me in middle-class Jewish American life in the fifties. With the effects of this unexpected reminiscence pressing in, I commented with a slight edge, gazing at his not inconsiderable gut, surprising in a trainer: "Well, if you go around saying things like that, I hope you're Jewish." Actually, T.W. confessed, he wasn't; his ex-wife, who was, had taught him the expression. We completed the tour of the machines without further conversation. Swimming afterwards, I reviewed the episode with the obsessiveness brought on by doing laps. What kept coming back between strokes was less my lame reply than the thought of the figure I must have cut in his eyes, the image that had led him to make the association: a middle-aged Jewish woman who needed to work on her triceps.

Here's the plot summary Spiegelman offers the reader at the beginning of the second volume of the *Maus* books: "Art Spiegelman, a cartoonist born after WW II, is working on a book about what happened to his parents as Jews in wartime Poland. He has made a series of visits to his childhood home in Rego Park, N.Y., to record his father's memories. Art's mother, Anja, committed suicide in 1968. Art becomes furious when he learns that his father, Vladek, has burned Anja's wartime memoirs. Vladek is remarried to Mala, another survivor. She complains often of his stinginess and lack of concern for her. Vladek, a diabetic who has suffered two heart attacks, is in poor health." What Spiegelman doesn't say—because it is immediately visible in the pages of the book itself—is that as a cartoonist he *draws* his book and that in it the Jews are portrayed as mice, the Germans as cats, the Poles as pigs, and so on. What he also doesn't say is that in real time Vladek is dead. *Maus* is about talking with the dead, with parents still alive in our heads.

What does it mean to make art out of Auschwitz? To make money from a cartoon version of the Holocaust? Is it possible to represent in concrete physical terms a world designed to confound the human imagination? These are some of the large moral questions that *Maus* rehearses and displaces through a set of visual and literary choices. Spiegelman himself has weighed the risk the comic book format runs. Writing in the journal *Tikkun* after the publication of *Maus II*, Spiegelman worries that what he calls his "comix"—a hybrid form of narrative that "mixes together words and pictures"—may have given people "an easy way to deal with the Holocaust, to feel that they've 'wrapped it up.'" His strategy for crafting this challenge to the ethics and materials of popular culture is to personalize the enormity without reducing it. Spiegelman distills the experience of Auschwitz as an individual's trajectory and a family's saga, but the collective horror never ceases to haunt the horizon of a singular history. At the same time, in retelling that tale as a comic book, Spiegelman binds its meaning to the very process of rendering that material; in both cases, the process depends upon the father/son collaboration.

From the start of the Maus books there's a troubling ambiguity about whose story, not to mention what kind, it really is. History, documentary, biography? A son's biography of his father? A family memoir? On the cover of the first volume the reader encounters the portrait of the father/mother (mouse) couple. Although the son clearly distinguishes between the two lives and seeks to disentangle them, what he can know of his dead mother's experience is limited finally by the presence of his living father's words: "I can tell you"—Vladek gestures disparagingly—"she went through the same what me: *terrible!*" Nonetheless, from beginning to end, the question of

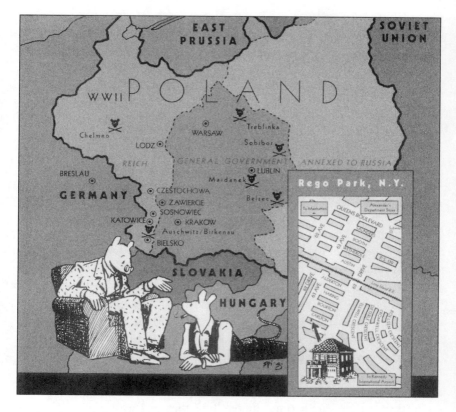

Anja's truth haunts Spiegelman's self-portrait as a son, an artist, and an ethical being.

Maus: A Survivor's Tale reconstructs a father's life, and as in *Patrimony*, the father/son relation provides the frame through which we gain access to the survivor's world. But two equally crucial differences separate the biographical projects of these Jewish American sons. In *Maus*, Vladek's story is inseparable from the historical world of the Holocaust. It is also inextricably tied to Anja, to his dead wife's fate. Art feels the absence of Anja's voice in the shape of his undertaking. Despite her silence, or rather because of it, the dead mother drives the narrative.

In the present tenses of Rego Park we are lured into the horrific account of a Holocaust past through the comforting banality of postwar American domestic life. Vladek pedals on an exercise bike in his son's former room and asks him about the "comics business." Art answers by recalling an old project of drawing a book about his father's life. Vladek discourages him: "It would take *many* books, my life, and no one wants anyway to hear such stories." But Art has already anticipated his resistance: "*I* want to hear it. Start with Mom. . . . tell me how you met." "Better you should spend your time to make drawings," Vladek protests, "what will bring you some money." From the start the father/son dialogue—about the Holocaust and about themselves—is entangled with these two powerful autobiographical strands: the son's self-portrayal as an artist and his relation as an artist and a son to his (dead) mother.

By the luck of generations in European Jewry, my family on both sides, like many families of the great waves of immigration from Poland and Russia in the late nineteenth and early twentieth centuries, "missed" the Holocaust. The lines of our history as Jews are shadowy, remote. Our geographies do not include the camps. For us, at the origin are only stories, no places. By this I mean that retrospectively where one came from is only a site without names—somewhere near Minsk. There is no home, only a place one left—a place marker, and not a place to which one would ever return, even if it could still be found on a map. I've often wondered whether the slightly fraudulent sense of Jewish identity I've always had wasn't bound up with the fact that my grandparents—three of whom I knew—seemed to come from places unreal to them. What counted finally were my maternal grandfather's perfectly retold stories about being drafted into the army, pogroms. From my paternal grandparents' side there were no stories, but a few artifacts: silver serving spoons and forks with family initials engraved in Russian letters. My grandfather's slim silver cigarette case. One of my father's cousins living in Canada told me recently that the silver came from their maternal family's tenure as caretakers on an estate somewhere in Kishinev; their name was Scholnick. No one seemed to have any hard information about ancestors, and no one seemed to care. It's with these scraps of information that I piece together my history. Fragments of a legacy about being Jewish—then.

.   .   .

"Time Flies" (the second chapter of *Maus II*) lays out the terms of Art's self-portrait as an artist in the context of the themes of vocation and commemoration. Wearing a mouse mask, Art gazes at his drawing board and thinks about his place in the double, alternating times of contemporary and historical memory: "Vladek died of congestive heart failure on August 18, 1982 . . . Françoise and I stayed with him in the Catskills back in August 1979." As the flies rising from the mound of mouse corpses buzz around his head, Art interweaves the threads of family histories: "Vladek started working as a tinman in Auschwitz in the spring of 1944 . . . I started working on this page at the very end of February 1987." Sighing (or is he just smoking?), he underscores the ironies of his project: "In May 1987 Françoise and I are expecting a baby. . . . Between May 16, 1944, and May 24, 1944, over 100,000 Hungarian Jews were gassed in Auschwitz. . . ." Then, addressing the reader, Art recalls his publishing history: "In September 1986, after 8 years of work, the first part of *Maus* was published. It was a critical and commercial success." Art groans under the fame *Maus II* (published in 1991) has brought him. "At least fifteen foreign editions are coming out. I've gotten 4 serious offers to turn my book into a T.V. special or movie. (I don't wanna.) In May 1968 my mother killed herself. (She left no note.) Lately I've been feeling depressed." From outside the frame, a disembodied bubble of words tries to get his attention for a television interview. "Alright Mr. Spiegelman. . . . We're ready to shoot. . . ."

After the scene with the media, Art heads uptown for a therapy session and dwells painfully on the effects on him, as a son and an artist, of living in simultaneous geographies and temporalities: in Poland and Rego Park, in Reagan/Bush 1980s America and in Poland, in your family's death trip and in your own paternity. Climbing onto the chair in the body of the small child that the interview session seems to have reduced him to—"I want . . . my *Mommy*! . . . *WAH!*"—Art complains about his creative block. (In the show about *Maus* held at the Museum of Modern Art, there's a drawing placed in counterpoint to the "Time Flies" panels that literalizes this metaphoric state: a self-portrait of the artist as a slightly

Time flies...

103

warped child's playing block, under which Spiegelman has written, "My projections of what others now expect of me from *Maus* have bent me out of shape. . . . They're not meetable." The block does look a little the worse for wear.) This crisis has to do with the effects of commercial success, in part with the nature of the project itself. It also has to do with his unfolding personal—if always familial—story. "I can't believe I'm gonna be a father in a couple of months.* My father's ghost still hangs over me." (The * signals the birth of his daughter, Nadja Mouly Spiegelman.)

How to finish telling the story and move on when the haunting of the past *is* your material? "Somehow," Art explains, "my arguments with my father have lost a little of their urgency . . . and Auschwitz just seems too scary to think about . . . so I just *lie* there. . . ." Pavel, the therapist, who is also a survivor of the camps, responds sympathetically. "It sounds like you're feeling remorse—maybe you believe you exposed your father to ridicule." "Maybe," Art replies. "But I tried to be fair and still show how angry I felt." At an appearance at the 92nd Street Y, in which Spiegelman and Jules Feiffer talked about their work, Spiegelman pointed out that Pavel is wearing a Vladek mask and commented, "That's what therapy's about." The audience laughed knowingly, as though they understood from experience the power of a father's mask and at the same time, as cultural critic Alice Kaplan puts it, the "haunting of personal history by the political." If we no longer can separate the personal from the political, it's also the case that therapy is the way the postwar generation "has learned to understand history."

I grew up on the Upper West Side of Manhattan in the late forties and early fifties. My sister and I walked past the Paris Health Club (then a hotel) twice every day, on our way back and forth between home and P.S. 75 (incongruously named the Emily Dickinson school). We grew up knowing we were Jewish but without any conscious awareness of what Jewish identity had meant historically in the world. Whatever I learned in Sunday school or absorbed through sheer repetition at the Seders—the years in the desert, the plagues—was radically disconnected from the

dramatic events of contemporary history, of which I managed to remain
ignorant for a very long time: World War II, the Holocaust, the creation of
Israel. I doubt whether these events were discussed in When the Jewish
People Was Young, *the only book we read in those weekly exercises in*
Reform Judaism for children whose parents could neither pass on the tradi-
tion themselves nor give it up. (Rereading Memoirs of an Ex-Prom
Queen, *I was enchanted to find a bond with Alix Kates Shulman's sar-*
donic midwestern heroine: "If there ever was a possibility that I might have
fallen for stories like Genesis or Moses and the Ten Commandments, it was
destroyed by the ridiculous title of the textbook we used: When the Jewish
People Was Young."*) To assuage their twin anxiety about religious*
assimilation (moving away from the un-American constraints of Ortho-
doxy) and social mobility (out of immigrant insecurity into professional and
business solidity), our parents insisted on the signs of a certain conformity to
the tradition. Sunday school was the perfect solution. From those years of
enforced attendance I retain mainly the title of that book—the singular
verb after "people" made an impression—and the Americanization of the
holidays as theme park: "Supersonic" Purim in the basement of Temple
Israel. That I thus officially became a Jew is recorded on a certificate of
"confirmation."

Our world was divided into Jews and non-Jews. Being Jewish had pri-
marily to do with knowing who else was and wasn't Jewish. Why that
mattered so much became clearer with puberty, which in my parents' apoc-
alyptic sense of timing led directly, leaping through the years, to sex (the
avoidance of) and marriage (the condition for the former): We had, they
said, to marry one.

Staying angry, being fair.

Maus emerges from the struggle between those contradictory
impulses. "Mainly I remember arguing with him. . . ." Art says in
a therapy session after his father's death, "and being told that I
couldn't do anything as well as he could." Pavel replies, focusing on
the public reception of *Maus*. "And now that you're becoming successful, you feel bad about proving your father wrong." That's not
quite it. "No matter what I accomplish," the son signs, "It doesn't

seem like much compared to surviving Auschwitz." Pavel works to
undo that double bind: "But you weren't in Auschwitz . . . you were
in Rego Park. Maybe your father needed to show that he was always
right—that he could always *survive*—because he felt *guilty* about
surviving. And he took his guilt out on *you*, where it was safe . . . on
the *real* survivor." Art leaves the session cheered up, ready to work
on the next panels, his father's stint as a tinman at Auschwitz, but his
"maybe" lingers unresolved. If his father, as Art puts it, "bleeds history," the son draws blood. Maybe the only way to prove your father
wrong is to retell his story, throw his voice, take off his mask.

The success of *Maus* is due in part to a double audacity. The first
is the choice to represent the Holocaust as a cartoon. The second, to
cast its star witness—the survivor without whom the artist would
never have visualized this cataclysm of history—as a victimizer in
his own world, a petty tyrant at home. What belongs to History, to
the world of public event, and what to family history, to the private?
The anger Vladek inspires in his son is palpable in the narrative
frames in which Vladek's post-Holocaust manias are thoroughly
detailed. Art and Mala discuss the effects of Vladek's stinginess.
While sympathizing with Mala, Art wonders aloud whether it was
the war that made him the way he was. "*Fah!*" Mala dismissively
counters, "*I* went through the camps. . . . *All* our friends went
through the camps. *Nobody* is like him!" If Vladek's cheapness—Art
tries calling it "pragmatism"—is unique to him and not due to the
war experience, then what is its explanation? "It's something that
worries me about the book I'm doing about him. . . . In some ways
he's just like the racist caricature of the miserly old Jew." To Mala's
emphatic assent, Art adds, "I mean, I'm just trying to portray my
father *accurately*! . . ." But for a cartoonist who works in a medium in
which accuracy is often an effect of exaggeration, the relationship
between accuracy and caricature is a vexed one, especially if the son
is still angry at his father.

Suddenly, interrupting Mala's lament, Art invokes Anja: "I wish I
got *Mom*'s story while she was alive. She was more *sensitive*. . . . It
would give the book some balance." But Anja's view of Vladek might
not redeem him either. "Your mother," Mala replies sympathetically.

"I just don't know how she could stand living with him. . . . I don't know how *I* can stand it!" How could Anja stand it? Maybe she couldn't. Anja's suicide was the subject of a four-page sequence entitled "Prisoner on the Hell Planet: A Case History," published thirteen years earlier, as Art puts it, in "an obscure underground comic book." Why reprint it now? By including the previous version of Anja's death in *Maus*, Art distances his adolescent self (both survivor and victim of his parents' life story) from his current project. By republishing "Prisoner" in the context of the parental biography as well as in the internal narrative of *Maus*'s production (we learn as we read how the book is being made), Spiegelman also insists on what losing Anja meant *to him*. After all, a mother's suicide is at least as important to a son as a wife's suicide is to her husband—especially in a world of competitive suffering.

"Prisoner" is a case history for the annals of survivors' children. Set in *Maus*, the story makes another kind of sense, especially in the always unfolding history of trauma over time; and the emotional power of the full-scale memoir has a great deal to do with this incorporated—stylistically different—document. Mala, who was shocked, she says, when "Prisoner" first came out—"so *personal!*"—now expresses admiration: It was "very accurate . . . objective." Art also commits his father's approval to paper. He shows Vladek (who, Art complains, "doesn't even look at my work when I stick it under his nose") discovering "Prisoner" for the first time, and admitting that he cried. "It's good you got it outside your system," he says to Art. "But for me it brought in my mind so much *memories* of Anja. Of course I'm thinking always about her *anyway*." Vladek explains that he came across "Prisoner" while looking for the notebooks Art had asked him about. This connection leads the son back to his hunt. "Did you find Mom's diary?" he asks. "I've *got* to have that!" Vladek equivocates, adding to the first lie (looking for something he knew didn't exist). "So far this didn't show up. I looked but I can't find. Another time I'll again look."

Beyond the role that the quest for a mother's story plays in this particular family configuration, most children desire to uncover their parents' truth. Wanting to know their story is central to the desire for self-knowledge that also drives the autobiographical project: How can I know who I am if I don't know who they are? Put another way, what's missing is precisely what makes autobiography—and biography—different from fiction. If it's not knowable, it can't be made up. At least not without violating the ethics of the genre. Spiegelman addressed this issue when he protested the *New York Times*'s listing of *Maus II* on the fiction best-seller list. "As an author I believe I might have lopped several years off the 13 I devoted to my two-volume project if I could only have taken a novelist's license while searching for a novelistic structure." But even when the documents are there, mystery remains. Nonfiction does not guarantee that the enigmas of family history will be solved. But talking with the dead in pictures is Spiegelman's way of finding a new form for the unpresentable truths of a documented past.

My parents loved a certain number of jokes and stories that were told over and over again. In memory it seems as though they were repeated daily, usually to make a point. Mostly I retain the punch lines of the jokes, which in some cases I spent a lifetime not understanding. Even when I can reconstruct the sequence of a joke's unfolding, I never remember it well enough to tell for a laugh. I still can see my parents doubled over in tears, unable to contain themselves as they retold a story they had heard, interrupting each other for corrections, invariably ruining the joke in the process. When they explained the joke to my uncomprehending sister and me, they added that it was much funnier in Yiddish, which of course meant that the essence of the joke was lost—on us—in translation. This is one I never thought was really funny, though I did smile at its aptness when I heard it as an adult, in French—in Paris. (By then I was willing to be Jewish.)

> *Elderly lady on the Broadway bus to young man in the seat next to hers:*
>   "*Excuse me, young man, are you Jewish?*"
> *Young man, politely:*
>   "*No, I'm not.*"
> *After a pause:*
>   "*Are you Jewish?*"
>   "*No, I'm not.*"

*This exchange is repeated several times. Despite the consistently negative
answers she receives the old lady asks the young man one last time:*
   "Are you sure you're not Jewish?"
*Exasperated and hoping to put an end to the badgering, the young man
finally gives her the answer he thinks she wants:*
   "All right, yes, I'm Jewish!"
To which the old lady replies:
   "Funny, you don't look Jewish."

The republication of "Prisoner on the Hell Planet" in *Maus* explicitly connects the enigma of Anja's suicide to Spiegelman's task as an
artist—but also as the child of survivors—of the Holocaust. The
specter of her dead body constitutes a crucial piece of the *Maus*
recovery project: a son's doomed but also belated attempt to get his
mother's story, a story that can neither be separated from nor fully
explained by historical event. What did your mother want? In the
penultimate episode of "Prisoner," Art turns away from his mother's
plea—"Artie . . . you . . . still . . . love . . . me. . . . Don't you?"—and
fantasizes that this rejection makes him responsible for her suicide;
the image of his mother in pained retreat locks him figuratively into
the jail of his guilt, fed by the imagined hostility he heard in the
condolences of his father's friends. "Arthur—we're *so* sorry." "It's his
fault, the punk." But is suicide a matter of blame? And which victim
should be blamed?

   Drawn into the title frame of "Prisoner," a hand holds a summer
snapshot of Anja and Art dated 1958 (ten years before the suicide).
It's hard to make out the expression on the mother's face. Art is grinning at the camera. Like mother, like son? He identifies with his
mother, whom he is said to resemble: "Always Artie is *nervous*—so
like his mother—she also was nervous"; like his mother, we learn in
"Prisoner," he has spent time in a mental hospital; and he looks like
his mother's brother, "a sign painter, a commercial artist, always she
said you resemble." (He killed himself, too.)

   Being like Anja, looking like her brother, looking that is to say,
Jewish. When Vladek and Anja begin the wanderings that land them
willy-nilly in Auschwitz—caught in the "mouse trap"—they put on

Polish pig masks as protection. Vladek worries less about himself, since he has put together an outfit "so like a Gestapo wore when he was not in service," but for Anja, passing is trickier: "Her appearance—you could see more *easy* she was Jewish. I was afraid for her." In the "Prisoner" photo of mother and son, Anja rests her hand on Artie's head; the hand that a few panels later will hold the razor blade. Replaced in the *Maus* books, Anja's suicide is given not an explanation but other narratives through which to reach it; her story—their picture—is forever part of his.

In a single panel Spiegelman renders the impossibility of ever knowing the answer to the "why" of his mother's suicide. Anja lies naked in a tub, under which thick capital letters spell out "MENO-PAUSAL DEPRESSION." A triangle of concentration camp iconography—barbed wire, piled-up human corpses, a swastika, under which "HITLER DID IT!" is scrawled—separates the body in the tub from the jarring scene below. Beneath the tub, three images are juxtaposed. A mother reads in bed with a little boy dressed in miniature prison garb by her side, "MOMMY!" A forearm with concentration camp numbers on it slits a wrist with a razor blade, "BITCH." The jumble of words and images constructs a mosaic of truth that resists any single interpretation.

What more would the son have learned about his mother from her memoirs? After Vladek has told the inaugural story of the persecutions in their town, Sosnowiec—the hanging of four Jews for dealing in goods without authorization—Art asks what his mother was doing in those days. "Houseworks ... and knitting ... reading ... and she was writing always her diary," his father answers. "I used to see Polish notebooks around the house as a kid. Were those her *diaries?*" "Her diaries didn't survive from the war," Vladek explains. "What *you* saw she wrote after: Her whole story from the start." *Her whole story from the start.* "*Ohmigod!* Where are they? I *need* those for this book!" The paternal narrative in *Maus I* ends with Anja's and Vladek's arrival at Auschwitz, but the framing text—the conversation between Art and Vladek—that concludes the volume itself reveals how in a second holocaust Vladek burned the notebooks in order to put that past behind him: "these papers had too many memories." Art explodes, furious at the destruction of his mother's "wartime memoirs"; Vladek blames the depression that followed Anja's suicide for his act. In the last panel, Art walks off, smoking his eternal cigarette, and convicting his father: "Murderer." We have seen this accusation before. At the end of "Prisoner on the Hell

Planet" Art draws himself in jail, calling out to his mother, "Congratulations! . . . You've committed the perfect crime. . . . You *murdered* me, Mommy, and you left me here to take the rap!!!" "Prisoner on the Hell Planet" is about the rage of surviving the survivors. In *Maus* the survivor performs an act of reparation.

If the first volume of *Maus* begins with a son's betrayal (Art draws what he has promised Vladek not to tell), it ends with the exposure of a father's lie, or rather with his confession. When Art asks his father whether he can remember what Anja wrote in her notebooks, Vladek answers that Anja had expressed the hope that her son would value her bequest: I know that she said, 'I wish my son, when he grows up, he will be interested by this.'" In a way, then, the mother got her wish; her son turned out to be passionately interested in her experience at Birkenau, in what happened to her when the inseparable couple arrived at the great gender divide of the camps. "And when they opened the truck, they pushed men one way, women to the other way. . . . Anja and I went each in a different direction, and we couldn't know if ever we'll see each other alive again." In the second volume of *Maus*, when Art tries to bring Vladek back to this moment, Vladek goes back on his own words: "But you understand, *never* Anja and I were separated!" No? Art asks, puzzled. "*No!* The war put us apart, but always before and after, we were together." This erasure is the wok of trauma. To destroy the diaries is also to wipe out the proof of their separation, the suffering Vladek could not endure, the suffering beyond his control. The murder of memory tries to make loss bearable. But as it turns out, it's only the restructuring of memory that gives loss its rightful place. The urgency of that countermemory is what animates Art's project in *Maus*. In the scenes of life in the concentration camps that follow the therapy session, Vladek relates what he managed to learn of Anja's fate while she was interned in Birkenau (Auschwitz II). He quotes from memory a letter, testimony to Anja's despair: "'I miss you,' she wrote to me. 'Each day I think to run into the electric wires and finish everything. But to know you are alive it gives me still to hope. . . .'" Despite the "reproduction" of the letter—the only instance of Anja's written words we have—we are left with a voice mediated by multiple modes of translations: into Vladek's English (from her written Polish—"Almost nobody could write Polish like she wrote," Vladek had boasted earlier), into his spoken English, into Art's transcription of the tape, into the visual version of the transcript, into his idealized version of the couple, into Art's comic strip. In whatever language, Anja's voice delivers the message of despair that seems to have been hers from the start. (Snooping around in his future bride's house, Vladek finds pills that make him worry about the deal he is getting—Anja's family is very rich and eager for her to marry. But he accepts the explanation of a druggist friend that "the pills were only because she was so skinny and nervous." In the early days of their marriage, after the birth of her first son, Richieu, Anja suffered a nervous breakdown and spent three months being treated in a luxurious sanitarium in Czechoslovakia. As usual, Vladek assigns himself a key role in her restoration, telling jokes and stories. "I understood much of such sicknesses, so I helped always to calm her down.") The *Maus* books point to everything we can't know but can guess about a woman's life that ended in suicide—with no note.

In the all-American fifties, not looking Jewish, we thought, was more important than being Jewish. By junior high, when looks are all, I had come to understand that looking Jewish was bad, aesthetically. (We had crushes on the counselors at summer camp. Blond, cheerful, long-legged phys ed majors—our vulgar parents, to our horror, referred to them as "shiksas"— they embodied all that we intense dark-haired campers would never be.) How did that deficiency of beauty square with what I had been told about being Jewish as something good—smarter, more talented, more sensitive? It didn't. Being smart and talented was taken for granted in the tracked classes and special schools (which served as the alternative to private school) for the "intellectually gifted" children, as the phrase went. In the fifties, middle-class parents thought of themselves, however apolitically, as belonging to the Left—and to prove it, didn't move to the suburbs. Being smart— and how smart could one be with "geniuses" everywhere (staggering IQs were routinely alluded to and boasted about)—seemed a poor consolation prize in the perpetual popularity contest that passed for life.

Girls like me obsessed about our appearance (alternately our "personalities") with a single-mindedness that closed out the larger world. (According to Seventeen *magazine, which we started reading at twelve, personality could make up for a less than perfect face or figure.) I wanted hair that moved. This was the era of ironing one's already straight long blond hair, glamorized by the whiter than white model Carol Lynley, to make it even more perfect. My father, whose dark, kinky hair I had inherited, signed a promise to me when I was nine that at age twenty-five I would no longer hate my hair. I was of course unmoved by his confidence—would I still be alive at twenty-five?—and talked my mother into letting me have my hair straightened once, just to see. But his prediction in fact almost came true: By 1968 I had a "natural"; my hair, briefly, was in. Despite my abject embrace of these aesthetic norms, whose historical significance I did not begin to suspect, like a George Eliot heroine I also nourished a nameless and secret wish for some way of being in the world outside convention altogether; it would take feminism and the sixties for me to discover what that was. In the fifties, our corner of the diaspora (a word I didn't know then) was a lonely place. We assimilated American girls, oblivious even to Anne Frank (represented in the movies, of course, as* not *looking Jewish) managed not to know that looking Jewish could mean death.*

At one point in *Maus II*, interrupting Vladek's narrative about the final days in Auschwitz, Art inquires about a Frenchman who helped Vladek in the camps, whether he saved any of his letters. "Of *course* I saved," his father answers. "But all this I threw away together with Anja's notebooks. All such things of the war, I tried to put out from my mind once and for all. . . . Until you *rebuild* me all this from your questions." For Vladek, "rebuilding" memory means reviving the link to Anja; Anja cannot be separated from the war: "Anja? What is to tell? Everywhere I *look* I'm seeing Anja. . . . From my *good* eye, from my *glass* eye, if they're open or they're closed, always I'm thinking on Anja." But this memory is by now the artist's material as well. Despite Vladek's protest, Art finally extracts the images he needs from his father's repertoire in order to close his narrative, including Anja's last days in Sosnowiec and their reunion: "More I don't need to tell you. We were both very happy and lived happy, happy ever after." The tape recorder stops.

Throughout the telling of *Maus*, Art forces Vladek back into the past of suffering and the double loss of Anja. In the corners of the pages Art presses Vladek to continue with his narrative until he pleads, "Enough." In real life Vladek dies before seeing himself reunited with his beloved Anja in his son's book, and before seeing his words and deeds in some ways turned against himself (though given his incapacity for self-criticism and his talent for self-justification, he would probably have missed the bitter ironies of his portrait). What would Vladek have made of his son's joking, on National Public Radio, about not wanting to be the Elie Wiesel of the comics?

During my graduate student years in France in the early sixties I discovered two surprising things: Jews who weren't American and ordinary anti-Semitism. I got to hear my first anti-Semitic remarks from French people who seemed to think that because I was American, I wasn't Jewish. I heard things that my life in the stylistically Jewish community of New York had sheltered me from, and I flirted with another kind of passing. This was the desire for an escape I could not have named then, out of a New York Jewish female fate and voice. Speaking French, dressing French, was not so much a way of "passing"—since I quickly discovered it is impossible to pass as French—as a subconscious displacement of the more predictable intonations of identity. At least that was the fantasy. The frisson of passing came in response to French people saying, "But you don't look American. You look . . . what are you really?" In this version, not looking American (Sandra Dee, Carol Lynley) was good; my French interlocutors were not thinking Jewish but something . . . different. Explaining that my grandparents came from Russia and Poland, though not mentioning the Jewish connection. I would add to my own pleasure by saying, "Oh, there are lots of girls in New York who look just like me." That no one seemed to believe me was the final touch of private gratification: my difference was unique.

·   ·   ·

The Museum of Modern Art show devoted to the making of *Maus* emphasized the work involved in the artistic, technical, and psychological process of converting paternal discourse into the visual and verbal languages of Spiegelman's comix. Located in the "Projects" room, the exhibition illustrated the detail of the Spiegelman method. In one display case the process by which Life becomes Art is broken down and narrated. "An incident from V. Spiegelman's transcripted memories becomes a page of *Maus*." A typed page of the transcript describing the long march out of Auschwitz is displayed and marked. The episode involves the shooting of a prisoner, which Vladek likens to a childhood memory of a mad dog being shot by its owner: "And now I thought: 'How amazing it is that a human being reacts the same like this neighbor's dog.'" The commentary in the display case deals with Spiegelman's technical process: "The incident is broken down into key moments, first into phrases, then into visual notations and thumbnail sketches of possible page layouts." In the next stage, "phrases are rewritten, condensed and distilled to fit into the panels." (Sometimes rewriting goes the other way. On tape Vladek said simply: "How amazing it is that a human being is like a dog.")

The exposition of the myriad details involved in the transformation of the father's narrative of lived atrocity into the son's comic book underscores the degree of re-presentation involved in the *Maus* project and the skills required for its realization. This is where despite their differences the boundaries between father and son sometimes turn out to be more permeable than distinct. The crossover works in complicated ways. Vladek, for instance, draws. In *Maus I* Art reproduces Vladek's detailed sketch of the bunker he designed for hiding in Sosnowiec: "Show to me your pencil and I can *explain* you . . . such things it's good to know exactly how was it—just in case." And Vladek likes to emphasize their commonalities; they have, he insists, the same hands: "Like you, Artie, my hands were always very delicate." But Art claims that he became an artist in part to define his identity *against* his father's. He hates his father's display of versatility, his ability and determination to know how to do *everything*. "He loved showing off how *handy* he was . . .

and proving that anything *I* did was all wrong. He made me completely neurotic about fixing stuff.... One reason I became an artist," he concludes "was that he thought it was impractical—just a waste of time.... It was an area where I wouldn't have to compete with him." At the same time, the exhibit lays bare the sheer manual dexterity entailed in the "comics business." Art had to learn to *draw* what his father had faked in the camps: how, for instance, to pass yourself off as a shoemaker when you're a (fake) tinman. Vladek explains that in the camps he justified his boast of having been a "shoemaker since childhood" (in reality he had watched his cousin work in the ghetto cobbler's shop). He describes repairing a lace-up boot in need of resoling. In the show, the technical drawing of shoe-making from which Art derived his cartoon version is mounted above a sketch from *Maus*. Vladek points out the moral of his suc-cessful gamble: "You see? It's good to know how to do *everything*." (A *New York Times* article on the adaptability of Holocaust survivors is illustrated by this same drawing of the shoe.)

In the therapy session, Pavel argues that survival in the camps was a matter of chance: "It wasn't the *best* people who survived, nor did the best ones die. It was *random!*" But Vladek's sense that he in some way made his survival come about by his skillfulness—speaking English, repairing shoes—inevitably shapes the narrative from beginning to end, and his son respects that shaping vision. When Vladek deals with the Americans who have arrived in Europe as liberators, he traffics successfully in goods and services. "So we worked for the Americans and they *liked* me that I can speak English." They prepared him for the translation from survivor to immigrant by renaming him, Ellis Island style: "They gave to us food cans and gifts and called to me 'Willie.'" In Pavel's view, "Life always takes the side of life." Art defines himself against his father the survivor. Nonetheless, the survivor's skills honed in the camps are passed on to the next generation as a matter of artistic ingenuity. The son figures out how to draw what defied visualization, even beyond the father's powers of authorization. "You *heard* about the gas, but I'm telling not *rumors*. But only what really I *saw*. For this I was an *eyewitness*."

Survivors who become immigrants, immigrants who are also survivors. My maternal grandfather, renamed William (called Willie) Miller, was a survivor. Because a rich relative in Canada reneged on a promise to sponsor his education, instead of becoming an engineer (his dream), he became a tailor of men's suits and coats in Manhattan's garment district. According to family lore, which was unanimous on the subject, Grandpa was an unsung genius who should have made a fortune. He "invented" a wrist-alarm watch (with a mechanism that tapped your wrist at the desired

*hour), a design for making artesian wells, a waterwheel boat that hung
above the bathtub in winter and navigated the pool in summer. He managed to get a patent for the watch, but nothing came of it; patents were too
expensive to pursue. For us grandchildren, these were the things of legend.
Pop, as his children called him, believed that it was good to know how to do
everything (and he did seem to know); this was an article of faith that he
passed on to my mother. But I prided myself on my inability to do any of the
things my mother could do well: sew, bake, cook for twelve at the drop of a
hat (my father's litany of her accomplishments), drive, win tennis tourna-
ments, stand on her head (in yoga), wire lamps, repair sinks, do the double
acrostic in an hour without a dictionary, invest money, balance her checkbook "to the penny." Fear nothing.*

*In our family, there was a clear divide between the (maternal) Millers/
survivors and the (paternal) Kipnises/schlemiels. My father's father (a
bookkeeper and "a sweet man") was said to have died of disappointment; he
never adjusted to the New World. When he died, Grandma Kipnis, a
woman renowned for her vanity (she was said to have rejected a suitor
because of the cut of his boots—in this style of unforgiving judgment, I was
said to resemble her), never left the house again, except to go to the doctor's.
She did, however, continue to dye (my mother never failed to observe) her
much admired, auburn waist-length hair. For a long time, I thought I was
a Kipnis. That was because I was going on hair and intellectual pretension.
I learned to fear everything (dogs, cars, co-ops), get lost in my checkbook,
despise everyone (if you want to understand infinity, my father liked to say,
think of human stupidity).*

What is the relation between creating *Maus* out of his father's words
and finding images for the suffering maternal body? If the outra-
geousness of comic book truth is any guide, and what you see is
what you get, then we should understand the question of Anja both
as that which forever escapes representation and that which requires
it: the silence of the victims. Why do we write about the dead? To
tell the story only we can tell and therefore to keep the work of
memory alive. This is what keeps Art forcing his father back into the
memories he has tried to destroy. He makes his father remember
(murdering the murderer), but for whose benefit?

No matter how hard Vladek may try to throw away the reminders of memory—Anja's whole story from the beginning—Art brings it back, creates his father's memoirs out of the junk he's saved and the valuable things he's thrown away. On some level Spiegelman offers up the dramas of saving and throwing away as a domestic allegory for the autobiographical project. Here and not here. Lost and found. The father's memory passed through the grid of the son's documentation. Post-memory. Post-memory is what critic Marianne Hirsch has defined as the memory you inherit from another's experience that powerfully shapes your identity, but is not directly your own. What are the ethics involved in appropriating another's memory, converting oral testimony into a written and visual document (let alone a comic strip!)?

What happens, for instance, *between* the father's living voice and the son's postmortem rendering of it as test, post-memory? In addition to the source materials on view in the exhibition—photographs, technical drawings, and so on—a tape of the father's voice was made available to the listener curious to know what Vladek sounded like. A reader's desire to hear this voice is intensified by the presence throughout the frame narration of the tape recorder, as the mark both of their collaboration, even after Vladek's actual death ("Please, Pop, the tape's on. Let's continue. Let's get back to Auschwitz"), and of the testimony's authenticity.

When I listened to the tape I was surprised by an odd disjunction between the quality of the voice and the inflections rendered in the panels. *On tape* Vladek regularly misuses prepositions ("I have seen on my own eyes," "they were shooting to prisoners"), mangles idioms ("and stood myself on the feet"), pronounces "made" as "med" and "kid" as "kit," but the total *aural* effect, unlike the typically tortured *visualized* prose of the dialogue in the comic balloons, is one of extraordinary fluency. It's almost as though in "distilling" his father's language to fit the comic strip, the son fractured the father's tongue. By contrast, the voice on the tape has the cadences of a storyteller: it is smooth, eloquent, seductive. Is breaking the rhythms of that voice an act of violence or restoration, or both at once?

What the show at MOMA (not to mention the CD-ROM of *Maus*) allows to happen—which the text as visual representation necessarily forecloses—is that the reader of *Maus* gains momentary access to the voice that survived the event, freed from the printed diction of the frame. In that moment (and listeners greedily listened to every word of the tape, unwilling to relinquish the headphones), one is tempted to say, the father performs unmediated—to the world. But this would also be to miss the crucial function of the listener in the production of testimony. As Dori Laub writes in *Testimony*, "The listener . . . is a party to the creation of knowledge. . . . The testimony to the trauma thus includes its hearer. . . . The listener to trauma comes to be a participant and a co-owner of the traumatic event. . . . The listener, however, is also a separate human being . . . he preserves his own separate place, position and perspective; a battleground for forces raging in himself, to which he has to pay attention and respect if he is to properly carry out his task." Paradoxically, then, the reader's experience of the father's voice returns her to the son's task and its realization. As "co-owner" of his father's trauma, the son cannot fail to map out those places and those wars—the struggle between anger and fairness. By forcing Vladek to "rebuild" his memory, Art becomes both what Laub calls the "*addressable other*" necessary to the production of testimony and the subject of his own story. Whose story is it? Spiegelman created *Maus*, he explained in response to a question asked at his performance at the 92nd Street Y, "in order to remember my father's story by making it visible for myself." Like Roth in *Patrimony*, Spiegelman (whose name in German means "mirror-man") re-creates his father by creating him in his own image.

Grandpa Miles was a great storyteller. And his children, our parents, told stories about his stories: they memorialized the man and his life. In the summers when we were little, Grandpa would take the grandchildren out in his grey Packard and spend hours in the woods (probably bushes) telling us terrifying stories, real or made up, we never knew, of the Russia he had left behind. I can't remember a single one, but I still can conjure (all the cousins can) the powerful sense of being caught in the web of narrative, immobilized by someone else's words—someone else's life, in translation. Everyone in the family says that Grandpa had no accent ("he learned English in night school" is the ritual explanation for this), but when I hear him in my head, the "w" is always threatening to betray him, is always in danger of migrating into a "v." Maybe I kept hearing the immigrant he so clearly was in the music of his voice. In one of the home movies that record those summer days, the children come piling out of the car blinking into the sunlight as though returning from another world. Once "Pop" died, the bonds among the children and the grandchildren, ever tenuous, snapped. A summer patriarch.

The last drawing in *Maus II* is of the tombstone bearing the names of Art's parents as well as their birth dates and the years of their deaths (1968, 1982); beneath the monument the artist signs the dates that mark the production of his book: 1978–1991. The dates on the tombstone give the lie to Vladek's "happy ever after," since Anja killed herself some twenty years after the war. Did she live happy ever after? Mala, Vladek's second wife, doesn't mince words: "Anja must have been a *saint*! No wonder she killed herself." The dates also point indirectly to the fact that Art's text keeps his father as well as his mother alive. Both volumes of *Maus* were published— and critically acclaimed—after the death of the man who thought, after looking at some of his son's early sketches of the Jews hanged in Sosnowiec, that he might some day "be *famous*, like ... what's-his-name? You know ... the big-shot cartoonist...." "What cartoonist could *you* know? ... Walt Disney??" "YAH! Walt Disney." (The first four chapters of *Maus I* were completed by the time Vladek died.)

At the end of *Maus II* Vladek and Anja are together again—as they were in the penultimate panels of Vladek's narrative—only dead. Curiously, readers are not given access to the event of Vladek's death; it is mentioned, commemorated, but not represented. Art skips the funeral. Spiegelman wrote the last chapter of *Maus I*, in which he throws Vladek's lie about the diaries in his face and calls him a murderer, after Vladek's death, but in *Maus II* the son gives the dead father the last word of their dialogue. In his exhaustion from the past brought into the present, Vladek calls Art by the name of his dead brother. "I'm *tired* from talking, Richieu, and it's enough stories for now." The replacement child, the remaining son, replaces those ghost stories with the story of his making as if he could reframe a history he can't master.

Is the biography of another ever a story separate from ourselves? Is autobiography ever a story separate from the significant others— parents, lovers—with whom we continually make and remake our selves?

Taken together, the *Maus* books embody a son's knowledge about his father, mother, and history. Forged in the time of writing and drawn through his reconstruction of that material, they also wind up embodying him. In almost every frame in which Art appears, a lighted cigarette signals his presence. Like Spielberg's opening logo in *Schindler's List* of smoke rising from a ceremonial candle, an image that prefigures the relentless arithmetic of bodies going up in smoke (the chimney was a code word for the vanishing act of the millions), Art insists on his own powers of destruction. Vladek pedals on his Exercycle in Artie's former room. For exercise, Art lights up. (Is it only my ex-smoker's moralizing self-consciousness that fixes on this image as a signature? "You reek of tobacco," my mother would say, when she greeted me at the door on my visits home.) Vladek traded cigarettes for food in the camps; Art signs his postwar identity with an ironic puff. Maybe there's no way to survive the survivors without reenacting the price of survival on one's own body. Smoking gives you more than a fair chance at personal disaster.

The story of Jewishness that began in my grandparents' families ends with me. I watch with some wonder the parade of Orthodox Jews in my neighborhood. The groups of men of all ages in black or business suits, some with extravagant hats; the women, especially the younger ones, with their modern wigs (or fashion-proof hats), long skirts, and growing brood; the little boys with curling forelocks and skullcaps, the little girls in long dresses from another century and world. They seem unembarrassed by the spectacle they make (I'm embarrassed in their place). They have, after all, chosen it (and anyway, who are they to me?). I find these marks of belonging, like the legendary arms of the Hadassah ladies, both alien and familiar, but, I insist, not me. Still, the trainer at the Paris gym couldn't tell the difference. Who is it who gets to decide who one is?

In a way, *Patrimony* and *Maus* tell the same story: what it means to be a Jewish American son who makes art out of (and over) his father's dead body. Torn between two biblical commands—to bear witness and to not violate a father's sense of privacy—the sons choose to bear witness. They choose, that is, themselves. This is an ethic that allows the sons to publicize intimacies in order to make everything "more real," and that requires betrayal. The betrayal of secrets is a requirement of the autobiographical act. To mark off your difference through betrayal—you may be the father, I'm the writer—is the confirmation of both separation *and* relation. For autobiography is about who we are in relation to the other, alive and dead, father and mother. That broken bond is essential to the making not only of autobiography but of history.

When Spiegelman draws himself in the pages of *Tikkun* post-*Maus* with the ghosts of the hanging Sosnowiec Jews behind him, his daughter is sketched in at his feet—with Mickey Mouse in her lap, and drawings of her own on the floor. The next generation (as well as those previous)—is included in a self-portrait. The son places himself as a father under the sign of a collective fate. The man in the mouse mask moves beyond his listener's task by turning testimony into a story of his own making and placing his personal narrative in the weave of that history. But this is not to say that his losses, any more than those which define the survivor's life during and after Auschwitz, are erased by that gesture: Anja will not return to explain herself. Nor can he know to what extent his daughter, Nadja—whose name is an almost perfect anagram of Anja and to whom (along with his dead brother, Richieu) *Maus II* is jointly dedicated—will be free of *her* father's story. And yet by telling their interwoven story to a public outside the family, the son moves on beyond its constricting plot. Asked at the end of an interview whether he forgave his father for what he had done to his mother's diaries, Spiegelman replied, "Yeah, although I don't think it's my place to forgive or condemn. I guess I forgive him." If after the Holocaust violence and reparation can no longer be separated, perhaps this is also the form postmodern forgiveness takes.

With my father, 1945.

5

OUTING THE DEAD

I think at some point I looked at my father
and thought *He's full of shit.*
SHARON OLDS, "Waste Sonata"

I am amputated, inconsolable. My father has died.
Now I must invent him, perhaps fictionalize,
   mythologize him.
Most of all, I will have to find a way to mourn him.
E. M. BRONER, *Mornings and Mourning: A Kaddish Journal*

"When I began making a living as a journalist," Susan Cheever
recalls in the preface to *Home Before Dark*, "my father suggested that
if something disturbed me, I might try writing about it." The memoir is an effect of her father's advice. "In the autumn of 1981 when
we found out that my father was going to die soon, it seemed natural
that I should write about this." *Home Before Dark* began as a book
about the illness, about cancer and hospitals, about life in the present, but the claims of the past soon became too pressing to ignore.
"Everything that happened seemed to release a flood of memories of
our life together." What started out as a "slim volume of anecdote
and remembrance" turned into an undertaking of emotional retriev-
al in which the daughter willy-nilly becomes her father's biographer,
and in the process, finds out more than she bargained for.

"My father was always a storyteller." The stories her father tells
are what allowed him to make a living; they also indelibly shape the
ideas the family comes to have about itself. Susan Cheever carries
not only the Cheever story she inhabited but the twin burden and
gift of John Cheever's fiction, letters, and diaries in which she some-

times figures. These pages play a crucial part in her attempt to make sense of the story not told in fiction but in life—a life available to her only in paper, when its author is gone. Rewriting the life story of a *famous* parent edges the project perilously close to the zones of celebrity biography: the monument cut down to size, captured— infamously—in *Mommie Dearest*. No more than the writer, the reader of *Home Before Dark* (described as "a biographical memoir of John Cheever by his daughter") never escapes the effects of the Cheever name. We can't help seeing the places where the daughter-biographer who bears the name in her own right pays the price exacted by the family plot—as a daughter and as a writer.

"I wanted to keep my father alive. I wanted to tell a writer's story." Susan Cheever describes "a friendly competition" between her and her father about titles. The title *Home Before Dark* was one Cheever himself had designs on. It evokes a story he used to tell about his youngest child, Fred, who "came back from playing with some friends, worn out and tired too, and when he saw Daddy standing there he ran across the grass and threw his little boy's body into his father's arms: 'I want to go home, Daddy,' he said, 'I want to go home.'" This was a story John Cheever liked to tell, but here Susan Cheever tells it and joins in its interpretation: "Of course he *was* home, just a few feet from the front door, in fact. But that didn't make any difference, as my father well understood. We all want to go home, he would say when he told this story. We all do." The longing for home was at the heart of John Cheever's life, and this is how his daughter writes it for him—laying claim to his title after all. There's not much explicit reflection in *Home Before Dark* about the nature of the dark that binds the daughter to her father, but throughout the memoir there are powerful hints about what keeps the writer's only daughter yearning for home as she stands poised at the threshold, a lonely figure in her father's shadow.

Returning to visit my father when he was alone and sick, I never felt sure whose home it was. My parents lived in what real estate agents in New York like to call an Edwardian 5 (as distinct from a Classic 6). A prewar floor plan of an affluent couple's life: one master bedroom with a bath across a hall, a living room, a dining room, a kitchen, and a maid's room with a half bath. After the Depression, aspiring middle-class families adjusted their sights: the dining room became the children's room, the maid's room, a dinette. Four people shared a bathtub. When my sister and I moved out, my parents reconfigured the apartment. We had our own keys, but did we still live there?

My father's house. Who is my father? He seems so unknowable, this man whose secrets I now seek to uncover. Something about fathers, dead or alive. So much of them that is never at home. In the last years his face, except for the bags framing his eyes, is taut and smooth. This look is one of the symptoms of Parkinson's disease, called the mask. The skin gets pulled tight across the skull, the lines in the forehead almost vanish. But against this perversely rejuvenated surface the eyes go prehistoric; unblinking, they stare out vacantly. Like the caricature of face-lift, the eyes belong to another chronology. Where's Daddy? Sometimes he's there. His eyes light up when I walk in and he says: "Hiya, love." I kiss him on the forehead. Then the eyes go dead again.

Susan Cheever's act of memory is caught in the silent web of the daughter's seduction. This is an emotional captivity that has nothing to do with the peculiar fate of having a literary parent. The daughter who believes—wants to believe—that she is special to her father, that she is her father's daughter, suffers from a longing that is stronger than love and maybe had nothing to do with love at all. You don't have to be the daughter of a famous father to identify with someone you will never be, however much you long to. In her essay "Father and Daughter," Jessica Benjamin describes a moment in a child's development toward independence in which she (or he) wants to imagine herself (himself) as a subject who desires; and at this point the child turns to what Benjamin calls the "exciting father," the father whose power (in conventional models of parenting like those of the white American fifties in which Mother stays home and bakes while Father goes to the office) lies "more in relation to the world outside, beyond maternal power." This father with whom girls identify—"the erotic father," the father (or utopianly, mother and father) who "represents the child's love of the world"—

can take daughters where they want to go and show them who they can be. This is also why we hope so much for their recognition of us, of the ways in which we are *like them*. Especially, when they have made a mark on the world—even when they are dead.

You don't have to be famous to be cruel, and sometimes indifference is enough. When John Cheever entered the last phase of his writing life, Susan Cheever explains, she too "began to make a living writing fiction." Her father seemed pleased when her first two novels were published, but he also worried: "he wanted me to have a more secure and happier life than he had had." A parent's wish for a child's happiness is so often proffered against the child's desire. ("Better you should spend your time to make drawings what will bring you some money" is how Vladek tried to discourage his son Artie in Spiegelman's *Maus*.) Our parents seem to be saying, It's *because* I want you to be happy that I don't want you to do what you want to do.

Weeks before his death, John Cheever is home, ill and cold, despite the warm days of June weather. The heater is on and he seems to want something done. Mother and daughter speculate that Cheever wants the heater off and maybe unplugged, since he always feared electrical appliances might be dangerous, even when turned off. The mother shuts off the heater; the daughter pulls the plug out of the wall. "My father lifted his head. . . . From his face I knew I had done the wrong thing. 'How clever of you, Susie . . .'" Riveted by the sarcasm that brings back a history of humiliations, Susie stands there defeated: "I had come out from the city to love him; I couldn't do it. . . . Nothing helped. He didn't love *me*, obviously; how could I love him?" But the memoir is embedded in a love that thrives without reciprocity; it also thrives on fear. "I was always afraid of my father." Needing recognition from a father who withholds it keeps alive the confusion of those feelings.

Who is the man behind the mask? The lone ranger. He lives alone now, but then? At night, my sister and I would listen to the radio, behind closed doors, when we followed baseball games and watched the newsreels from the amusement park on the Palisades, glowing in the night sky across the

Hudson River in New Jersey. Radio days of the late forties, early fifties. The Lone Ranger. The Shadow. Dragnet. We would get scared and stay up talking in the dark. Sometimes we scared ourselves without the radio. I would tell my little sister stories about how the sea monster was going to come out of the river and devour her. To reassure ourselves we'd call out for water: "Daddy, we're thirsty, bring us a glass of water." Over and over again in a relentless singsong, punctuated by giggles—"Daddy, Daddy"—until Daddy finally broke down, came shuffling in with two glasses, looking half annoyed, half amused. Our triumph over Mommy's irritated "No! Just go to sleep." He came! Now, of course, we were having to pee. We'd drink our water, run to the bathroom, and finally, exhausted by our victory, drift off to sleep.

In the closing chapters of *Home Before Dark,* where Susan Cheever deals with her father's last days, she recalls her beginnings as a writer. She had wanted to ask for a loan and take time off from work to write a novel and twice had a failure of nerve. "'He would have annihilated you,' my brother Ben says now when I ask him what I was so afraid of. In our family, no one ever asked for help." With a continent between them, the daughter finishes her first novel. Cheever congratulates her in a letter—"I think that to complete a novel is a great accomplishment"—and then goes on to chat amusingly about her dog, whom she has left behind in his care. "When he read my novels," Susan observes with little emotion, "he was polite but perfunctory. 'I liked it very much,' he would say, or 'I thought it was fine.'" They dealt with the question of her vocation, she explains, by not talking about "the writing part of writing," just dealing with the business end of the profession.

But what did her father *really* think of her work? After John Cheever's death, his daughter has access to his journals, where she finds an entry written the day of the letter about her novel. The entry, "brief and equally enigmatic," concludes: "Ben ran the marathon in 2:59, in the 800 group among 11,000 contestants. Susie has completed a novel. None of us, particularly me, are first rate but we do, I like to think, persevere." If her father never says directly what he thinks of her work, his silence speaks volumes. While the publicity for her first novel is about to be released, Cheever writes in a letter: "WNET is rerunning the Cavett interview where I thank you for having made it so easy for your parents to love you. This brings up my gratefulness to you for the tact you've displayed in embarking on a literary career. Your independence has been peerless." There are expressions of love one can only be grateful never to have received.

Becoming someone. "*Marry and become a high school teacher, so you'll have something to fall back on in case your husband needs you to help out," my mother said. "Marry someone nice," my father chimed in. "Marry someone interesting," my mother added, "someone creative," but—the crucial caveat sealed the fantasy—"with an independent income." This was the kind of advice handed out routinely to smart girls who didn't know what to do with their brains and their desires. Marry . . . but. Impossible advice to follow, as it turned out, for an entire generation of women who later became feminists.*

Growing up, we never understood what my father actually did as a lawyer, although the materials of the profession were familiar and decorated the apartment: the yellow lined legal pads, the onionskin paper that crackled to the touch, the accordion-pleated folders. I've inherited my father's love of these materials, and my office now resembles his. "Every surface covered," my sister mutters in mock derision, as she tries on my mother's standard crack about my father's office. "There's no place to sit." But if I so resembled my father, why did it never occur to anyone that I should become a lawyer too? I asked my mother this in the seventies when women starting going to law school in droves and I started rethinking the plot of my life. Oh, Daddy had no respect for "lady lawyers."

I didn't do any of the things I was meant to do (find a husband to support me, have children, be happy) and none of the things I did (get a Ph.D., write books, have students) meant much to my parents. I brought them neither grandchildren (which my mother denied wanting: "don't expect me to baby-sit") nor proof that I was happy doing things my way (smoking, drinking, falling in love with unsuitable men, and flirting with suicide).

.   .   .

The question of becoming someone who goes out into the world gets complicated when, like Susan Cheever or Lynn Redgrave, you have chosen to follow your famous father's profession. *This is Living* is a hybrid form exemplary of postmodern culture in which Lynn Redgrave revisits her relationship with her actor/father: part autobiography, part self-help (how to overcome overeating through Weight Watchers), part recipes. The first section, "My Story," supplies a great deal of the material she used as a performer in the successful Broadway production of *Shakespeare for My Father*. A one-woman performance, it's the story of becoming an actress in spite of her father. Shakespeare for myself.

Like Susan Cheever's *Home Before Dark*, *Shakespeare for My Father* is an elegiac portrait of a publicly glamorous and internationally known figure. (Sir Michael Redgrave, C.B.E., is listed in "Who's Who in the Cast," and throughout the production a blown-up image of the father's face hovered, ghostlike, over the stage.) The daughter eulogizes her father as actor and rehearses—as an actress and a daughter—her place in his crowded schedule.

> My Godmother Edith is coming to school with Daddy to see me as Theseus in *A Midsummer Night's Dream*. I'm thirteen, shaking with nerves. Daddy never comes to concerts or school recitals. I'm sure he'll think I'm good as Theseus, I've worked very hard at it. I fantasize about his post-performance comments. "Brilliant, Lynny!" "I never knew you were so talented!" "You spoke so well!" "You looked just like a duke."
>
> Miss Borchard, my teacher, whispers, "Your father's just arrived. Middle of the fifth row."
>
> The stained blue velvet curtains in front of our little stage part, the audience murmur quiets, just a few squeaking chairs. I speak first, my arms around Harriet, who's playing my Amazon Queen.
>
> "Now fair Hypolita, our nuptial hour draws on apace . . ." My voice feels strong and manly, the scene playing so well.
>
> During the first Titania scene, I peek through the curtains to see how Daddy is reacting. His seats are empty.

What *does* Daddy think?

Beyond their fame, the Redgrave and Cheever fathers share a biographical profile: Both were bisexual, married to beautiful women, and parents of three children (Lynn and Susan were both born in 1943). All three of the Redgrave children are actors; two of the Cheever children are writers. These fathers, of roughly the same generation, with very different private styles, were equally difficult characters within the family: self-absorbed, remote, often cruel, though perhaps unintentionally. The daughters rework their relations with their fathers as they grapple in retrospect with their desire to be recognized by these monumentally self-involved men— not only as daughters deserving of love but as professionals worthy of paternal esteem. Their counternarrative isn't always powerful enough to break the hold of the father's claim to fame.

Susan Cheever addresses the question of her father's celebrity in the context of an interview she conducted in 1977 for *Newsweek* following the publication of Cheever's novel *Falconer*. "A Duet of Cheevers" (Susan Cheever then is Susan Cheever Cowley, married to the son of another famous father) follows a celebration of Cheever's work entitled "Cheever's Triumph," which reviews the novel and the career. The daughter interviews the father, but both prepared written questions; from the interview the reader has no way of knowing which ones. Cheever also provided answers. This is one of his questions, identified as such in the memoir but not published in the interview: "Do you think that the children of writers are destined to lead tragic and sorrowful lives?" The conclusion to her father's answer points to the great unspoken anguish beneath the smooth surface of the daughter's story: "It seems to me that anything you don't do yourself is very hard to handle. Any fame that comes to you, any money that comes to you, any talent that comes to you, you can't feel you've won yourself." It cannot be simple to write as Susan *Cheever*, to act as Lynn *Redgrave*. If *Home Before Dark* is a book only Susan Cheever could have written, the story behind its title is one that comes to her as part of a paternal bequest.

In the memoir, the daughter moves briskly from the interview questions to her father's diaries. John Cheever placed his journal writing in the context of a family custom. "Keeping ship's logs or journals and writing in general were part of our tradition." He used the same kind of notebooks that his father used. "The journals," Susan explains, "were private, of course, kept as a record of ideas and descriptive phrases as well as a means of writing some kind of order into pain and chaos." Nonetheless, like the diaries of so many well-known writers, they found their way into print. "I think," the daughter concludes, "he realized that the journals were an extraordinary document" and "he meant them to be read some day." But it is to his son, Benjamin, that Cheever puts the question of publication.

The Cheever children seemed to have resisted the temptation to read the typed pages filed in loose-leaf notebooks sitting on their father's desk for all the world to see. (In this tact, they resembled Jules-Joseph Colette's children who had observed their father's leather-bound volumes poised there ostentatiously on the upper shelves of the library, and never, it seems, thought to take them down.) Then suddenly a year and a half before his death, Cheever asked Benjamin, who was living at home after a failed marriage, to read one of the notebooks. He wanted to know "if I really thought there would be interest. I kept saying that there would be," especially for young writers. Was that enough of a reason to publish revelations certain to perturb his family, not to mention an audience of friends and readers? "Few people knew of his bisexuality," Benjamin observes in the introduction to *The Journals of John Cheever*. "Very few people knew the extent of his infidelities. And almost nobody could have anticipated the apparent desperation of his inner life, or the caustic nature of his vision." Benjamin Cheever diagnoses his father as suffering mainly—beyond alcoholism and its effects—from loneliness; he understands the diaries, in addition to the fiction and letter writing, as a way to "escape the loneliness, to shatter the isolation of others." He meant, the son concludes about the decision to make the private journals public, "to show others that their thoughts were not unthinkable."

The notion of writing so that others—in addition to oneself—will be less alone is always part of the autobiographical impulse. Journals, we tend to think, derive their value from the absence of a shaping interpretation; on the contrary we prize the insistence on the daily in its shapeless detail. Without the narrative force that comes from retrospection, the journal lacks a plot. But Cheever's journals have been edited with an eye to an audience of readers. And the excerpting from the great mass of pages, with entries reaching from the 1940s until the last days of his life, produces an autobiographical design. "When he discovered that he had written the story of his life," his son argues, "he wanted that published, too." What is that story? "He was a writer," his son maintains, "almost before he was a man."

Although the actual editing of the journals was done by Robert Gottlieb, the children were "collaborators" and active readers of these documents. Benjamin, who by his own account was the first child to be shown the journals and invited to read them, comments in his introduction: "The material was downbeat and often meanspirited. There was a lot about homosexuality. I didn't quite get it, or maybe I didn't want to get it. I was also surprised at how little any of us appeared, except my mother, who was not getting the sort of treatment that leads one to crave the limelight." Nonetheless, both as literary executor and the mother of these children, the writer's wife concurred in the decision to publish the diaries.

Home Before Dark and *Treetops* (the memoir about her mother's side of the family) were published before the diaries. In the first memoir, Susan Cheever recounts her discovery of Cheever's sexuality this way: "When my brother Ben told me that they were lovers," she writes of the relationship revealed in the diaries between "Rip" and her father, "I didn't listen, or I put the idea aside. It was only months after my father died, as I was reading his journals, that I found out. I guess what surprised me most was that I hadn't known." Despite the use of personal pronouns, she describes the love between the two men as if John Cheever were a man who belonged to another family: "His marriage to my mother was not particularly satisfactory, his children were gone, and his mistresses were old or in California. He also saw himself in Rip." The daughter treats their connection as though she were a biographer outside the story. In the logic of her own narrative, which is moving toward Cheever's death, this perspective makes sense: Rip was the person closest to her father in his declining years.

My sister and I always assumed that my parents were happily married. That's what they always said, despite all the bickering. There was that one period, though, in the early fifties, during which my father's career suddenly seemed to be taking off—he flew to California several times, kind of a big deal—when my sister and I sensed that something had gone seriously wrong. Somehow, we ferreted out the story. At least this is what we thought when I was thirteen and my sister ten. Daddy went to California and, one evening, riding up to his hotel room in Beverly Hills, made a pass at a woman my parents both knew from the summers spent in Croton-on-Hudson. When Mommy joined him in L.A., the woman told her she should put her husband on a leash. After that, Daddy was in the doghouse a lot. Especially whenever the subject of blondes with big boobs came up.

Looking back, Susan Cheever seems happy that her father had found love in this vulnerable stage of his life, and dwells briefly on her failure to read the signs in the face of her father's domestic roller coaster. "In a way," she offers by way of explanation for her failure to decipher the true nature of the bonds between the writer and his protégé, "I think the violent ups and downs of my father's life had exhausted all of us." *Home Before Dark* can be understood as a working through of the secret whose effects permeated the fabric of the family's life. But as a daughter, Susan Cheever refrains from naming the impact that reading the journals had on her. In particular, she glosses over the lie her father tells the world through her unwitting complicity in the *Newsweek* interview cited earlier. "Q. *Did you ever fall in love with another man? I mean, because of the homosexuality in "Falconer," people are certainly going to ask you that.* A. The possibility of my falling in love with a man seems to me to exist. Such a thing could happen. That it has not happened is just chance. But I would think twice about giving up the robustness and merriment I have known in the heterosexual world. Q. *Well, have you ever had a homosexual experience?* A. My answer to that is, well, I have had many,

Susie, all tremendously gratifying, and all between the ages of 9 and 11." Even the most casual reader of the Cheever *Journals* knows that this response is untrue in both the letter and the spirit. Elsewhere in the memoir Susan describes her father's struggle with homosexual desires as she learned about it from the journals. But here she keeps the fantasy of the "duet" alive, despite the fact that throughout this dark comedy, father and daughter are jarringly out of tune, as the passages excerpted from the *Journals* below clearly show.

> 1977. The present problem, if it is that, began a year ago when I found myself alone in a squalid motel with a young man who had none of the attributes of a sexual irregular. We embraced briefly, declared our love, and parted.
> 1978. Absolute candor does not suit me, but I will come as close as possible in describing this chain of events. Lonely, and with my loneliness exacerbated by travel, motel rooms, bad food, public readings, and the superficiality of standing in reception lines, I fell in love with M. in a motel room of unusual squalor. . . . When we met here, not long ago, we sped into the nearest bedroom, unbuckled each other's trousers, groped for our cocks in each other's underwear, and drank each other's spit. I came twice, once down his throat, and I think this is the best orgasm I have had in a year. We slept together, at his insistence, and there was some true pleasure here in discovering, I believe, that neither of us was destined to exhaust the roles we were playing.

The edited journals are packaged for readers as the record of one man's personal struggle with his demons and his ambitions. But placed within the memoir of a family they take on a subterranean force. Embedded in the context of the life around them and framed by the daughter who has read them whole, their relentless self-absorption makes the reader begin to feel how painful it had to have been to want something from the journal writer, a man so perfectly oblivious to the reality of others.

Cheever's interest in his daughter's writing seemed primarily a matter of numbers: "He developed a running literary score-card: Dumas (2), Bellow (1), Theroux (2), Updike (3)—both John

Updike's mother and son are published fiction writers—and exulted in our new parity." To be counted under the paternal signature by virtue of the numbers, rather than for oneself, was meant to be enough. This is not an uncharacteristic example of how John Cheever revealed, or didn't reveal, the complexity of his feelings toward his children: "We had wonderful times. A simpler way to put this is that my father loved his children. The three of us were, as he said, 'the roof and settle' of his existence. As individuals we often displeased him, but as a unit we were cherished and indispensable." Love dispensed generically is cheaper—and easier to give away. "He never spoke about feelings or allowed himself to speculate on the inner mechanics of the family. 'I love you all equally,' he would say, or 'I adore your mother.'" Cheever had a reputation for telling all—how much he drank before noon, what he was or wasn't paid for a story—but what a daughter thinks she most wants to know is consigned to silence. How much did her father love *her*?

Daughters especially seem to want to know what they meant to their fathers. Not only what they wanted from us, what they wanted *for* us. Lynn Redgrave opens *This is Living* with a vignette about returning home and finding herself alone with her father's memorabilia. Did she have a special place in his private thoughts?

I pick through a stack of papers and sit down by what is left of last night's fire. I read a letter or two and feel a little guilty. More photos, Mum and Dad in happier times. Dad in his many disguises—kings and common men, heroes, villains. Lear and Shylock. Hamlet, Uncle Harry.
Memories.
I shouldn't be looking, and yet this is my history, this is where I come from. This, I guess, made me what I am today. I allow myself a small laugh. . . .
Here. His journal for 1943—that's the year of my birth!
Apprehensively, I turn to my day, March 8th. A long, long entry. Last night's air raid. A day at rehearsal. A good performance in the play. . . . Who came round to see him afterward. An appointment at the Garrick Club.
But no birth. No Lynn.

Does your father even know you are alive?

By putting herself in the picture as a daughter and a writer, Susan Cheever sets out to re-create herself. After having been her father's creature in the journals and in the fiction, she invents a character who speaks in her own voice—or at least tries to. Rather than waiting for the public to read the revelations under her father's signature, she devises a new form through which to supply her view of his story, using his journal pages in her own book. Biographer and autobiographer, the daughter crafts an ambivalent critique of the author at home.

At a particularly successful moment in his career, Cheever composes a journal entry, imagining his twenty-year-old daughter's thoughts about her father's public accolades: "'After they put Daddy's picture on the cover of *Time*, he seemed to lose something. I don't mean like Dorian Gray or anything but like a savage who thinks that if he is photographed he will have lost part of his image.... Once I lost my temper at him and said I don't think anybody's impressed by the fact that you had your face on *Time* magazine.... They have all kinds of people; broken down ball players and crooks. It hurt his feelings, you could see.'" There are no more than a handful of journal entries in which Susan Cheever has herself appear in *Home Before Dark*, but this is the only one in which her words are invented. It's not surprising that this should occur around the theme of authorial vanity, the only one of Cheever's traits to produce an edge in the daughter's even (biographer's) tone. The daughter tends to forgive her father's sexual excesses more easily than his terminal narcissism. But at the same time she pulls back from her anger by including his hurt in it. Even if it's a hurt produced by his version of her!

In one of the final chapters we're given an acerbic portrait of Cheever as "his own number-one groupie." Infatuated with his persona as a successful writer—prizes, invitations, publicity—he tunes out the interlocutor at his side, looking expectantly toward the world at large: "Walking down Park Avenue with him once, after a lunch at the Four Seasons ('Che cosa di buona oggi?'), I noticed that he was smiling his public smile, at everyone who passed—just in case they recognized him, I suppose." But the cutting touch, after the Italian affectation, is saved for the end, when she comes upon her father at home glued to his Walkman, listening to himself read a story on tape. It's the perfect metaphor for Cheever's self-absorption in his late years—"listening, most of the time, to his own voice."

My father had few stories to tell. Once in a restaurant, pressed to supply some family history, he recalled his beginnings as a child of immigrants on the Lower East Side. He was born in the shadow of the Williamsburg Bridge. "I went everywhere on roller skates," he said, "even to Hebrew school," where that got him into trouble. Midway through the anecdote, he choked up and the tears started to flow, as they always did when he got to this part of the story. "Lou, pull yourself together," my mother hissed, "you're making a spectacle of yourself." My father took out his handkerchief and wiped his red eyes. End of story.

Once, my sister and I made a pilgrimage with my father to the old neighborhood. We wanted to see whether any memories would come back. He couldn't remember the address. Too much had changed. We gave up and went to Ratner's for lunch. Many years later, when I came upon some papers belonging to his parents and found the addresses, I discovered that the buildings he had lived in no longer existed. They had made way for schools, new housing. We had waited too long to find out.

"Appearances." At the center of the memoir, John Cheever's private fantasies about his daughter, about the woman he thinks he would like her to become, are revealed. "We were all told that appearances were not important, but no one believed it for a minute. My father described everyone and everything in terms of appearances." The example offered as illustration shows the extent of his preoccupation with how people and things looked. Cheever phones one evening to announce that "the most beautiful woman in the world" wants to marry him. How can you say no to such a request, he wants to know. "'You just do,' I said." After relating the episode of the phone call in all its glaring fatuity, his daughter moves on to the aspect of "appearances" that affected her directly when she was growing up. "Naturally, my father had expected his only daughter to be a beauty." But unfortunately her looks failed to live up to her father's hopes. Instead of getting the beauty whom he dreams of taking to the races at Saratoga or the Boston June Cotillion, as she discovers in his journals, his "Susie" is, in her own words, "dumpy, plagued by acne, slumped over." Overweight and brown haired, instead of the fair-haired heroine her father had counted on—"she'll have long blonde hair and drive a sports car and we'll call her Susie"—her looks, like her social life, disappoint.

Like the biographies of other celebrity figures, *Home Before Dark* contains photographs. "My mother was a beautiful girl," Susan Cheever writes of Mary Winternitz at the moment her parents meet, "just out of Sarah Lawrence, her brown hair streaked blond by the sun during the summer she had spent at Treetops." In the photographs the daughter resembles not her beautiful mother but her father—they share a face, a "Yankee face"; in the memoir, she identifies instead with his vocation. *Home Before Dark* is both capitulation and resistance to Cheever's power to reshape life through fiction.

Who is the girl with John? In Cheever *père's* fantasy everyone wonders enviously, when he turns up at the racetrack, "who the stunning young girl with John might be." He stages imaginary conversations with "the father of the groom—a Vanderbilt, a Biddle, a Cabot" in which he reassures "the old gentleman" that his daughter can handle the financial obligations that come with the territory. In this *echt* WASP fantasia, John Cheever gets to marry into the kind of family he seems to have wished he had come from; in his mind, he's suddenly on an equal footing with a Vanderbilt, a Biddle, a Cabot. It's a family romance in which you manage to be born into another setting, more in keeping with your idea of yourself. It's also a story about fathers and sons.

Mary Cheever's father—Dr. Milton Charles Winternitz, dean of the Yale School of Medicine—was Jewish. As Susan Cheever describes her grandfather's relation to his identity, "he never denied that he was Jewish . . . but sometimes he tried to forget it." He never tried to pass, change his name, or "transform himself into anything as pallid and bloodless as a WASP gentleman," but both the women

he married were Protestant and his children went to Sunday school
in the Congregational Church. There's a scene in *Treetops* in which
Mary Cheever, fed up with the anti-Semitic remarks Susan's sister-
in-law routinely makes in the course of a visit to the South of
France, intervenes with unusual passion: "I think you should know
that *I* am Jewish." The portrait of Winternitz and this moment of
self-identification are the only instances in which Jewishness figures
at all. It's as though that part of Mary's half has disappeared, swallowed up by the world of WASP gentlemen, the world in which John
Cheever fantasizes about his daughter marrying a Biddle (just as Dr.
Winternitz in a second marriage wedded a Whitney, the socialite
widow of one, rich in her own right). Despite an authorial remark in
the chapter devoted to her grandfather that we "live in an anti-
Semitic country," the essential WASPness of the Cheever universe as
the ultimate national idea and social ideal, especially in the but-
toned-down climate of the postwar fifties, is never brought to consciousness.

What's most striking about the land of the Cheevers is this easy
assumption of centrality: John Cheever's success as the quintessen-
tial *American* writer, before the emergence of hyphenated identities.
Perhaps the lively interest in the journals—whose revelations of
angst and homosexuality were on the whole well received—comes
from the disavowed desire of readers outside the magic circle to
know more about the cost of WASP privilege, what has to be kept
beneath the surface for the story to work. It's not that such violence
is absent from Cheever's fiction. On the contrary. But there's something about the geography of the memoir—the world *as* Westchester—that leaves outsiders, Jewish or otherwise, feeling as though
they are leafing through back issues of the *New Yorker* and puzzling
over the cartoons.

Appearances. As an adult woman with a marriage of her own to
negotiate, the daughter is impatient when her father, captivated by
his own, endlessly irresponsible love of "looking like something"
wants to marry the most beautiful woman in the world. But as the
narrator of her adolescent self, captured in retrospect, she has her-

self saying yes to an equally troubling fantasy: Despite her hopeless appearance, she will be her father's special companion. "As my friendship with my father deepened from our talks and going on trips or parties together—my mother was often too busy to go—the conflict over my looks intensified." If only she fixed herself up, lost weight, the right suitors would turn up. The temptation for a daughter to replace her mother (too busy!) as her father's friend and companion, to cast herself as a privileged interlocutor, is irresistibly heady for a girl with a literary imagination. Of course she will become a writer.

Father and daughter share a belief in literature. Talking about books and ideas, she writes, is their bond. It all began in Rome, where she turned thirteen and became a serious reader. "Our talks about Hawthorne were the beginning of the intense, often uncomfortable intellectual discussions I had with my father for the rest of his life. I began to read obsessively—all of Hawthorne, all of Balzac, all of Nancy Drew.... We talked about everything I read." Balzac *and* Nancy Drew? (The heroine for generations of American girls starting in the late twenties, Nancy Drew was, conveniently, motherless.)

Toward the memoir's close, Susan Cheever returns to the time in Rome for a metaphor of her father's final days. "When we lived in Rome, my father used to take me to outdoor concerts at the Basilica of Constantine. It was a romantic time for us—I was just thirteen that summer—and the most romantic of settings." Romantic. Father and daughter out walking as they did when she was little. Getting to be alone with your father when your mother is pregnant or too busy. He imagines you grandly married to a major WASP, so that he can play out his ideas of getting old with a stunning girl on his arm. Other men will admire him. You put yourself in your beautiful mother's place. The seduction of the "us" is everywhere in these pages—the family, the Cheevers, and the father/daughter couple—but the father/daughter "us" bathes in a special light.

In their journals, in their dreams, fathers and daughters try to figure out what they don't seem to want to know. The dark. "The dark," John Cheever writes in his journal when his nine-year-old daughter calls out for him before dawn, "'I have such awful thoughts, Daddy. . . . I think there is a tiger in the hall and that he will eat me.' . . . The dark is troubled for us both. There are no ghosts of men or tigers in the hall, but the dark is hard to bear." But of course it's not the same dark; this is the lesson of the journals. In the memoir, confusion of the paternal dark with a little girl's nightmare is followed directly by the event of that daughter's own motherhood. "On a cold sunny Monday, about two months before my father died, I checked into New York Hospital and had my own first child, a daughter, Sarah." The overlapping of love for first daughters—Susan and Sarah—almost breaks the hold of the dark, at least for the daughter telling the story.

John Cheever persists in the feeling of homelessness figured in the title of his daughter's memoir. "Twice since my return," Cheever notes two years before his death, "I have endured the sense of otherness. I am about to say to my daughter, sitting yesterday by an open fire, that I have returned home only to have refreshed the sense that there is no home, there is no surety or permanence in this world. I shut up." In the reproduction of entries like these, or through indirect accounts of other entries or conversations, the daughter casts herself as her father's privileged interlocutor. But when she revisits their history in the memoir, she can no longer not know that she's lived her life while in the dark.

As I was finishing this book, I decided to act the biographer and interview a few people who had known both my parents. I wanted to understand how their couple number had played in the world. My aunt—my mother's older sister—told me a story I had heard many times before about watching my parents fall for each other at a party, where they were meant to be introduced to suitable partners. They were both good looking and stylish, the bachelor and the maiden. But that was history, that was my parents before I was born. I was after something else.

I put my questions to an old friend of my parents who had known them as a couple since the late forties when they spent the summers in Croton-

on-Hudson, in Westchester. (My father commuted to the city; my mother played tennis and took my sister and me to the beach in the years before we went off to camp in the Adirondacks.) A painter, still sharp, beautiful and blond at eighty-one, she told me that in the early fifties my father had tried, as she put it, to "date" her. Years later, she added, her daughter confided that my father "had tried her too." More than forty years after the event, the memory is still fresh. The surprise, she said, was not so much the move—it wasn't gross or repeated, she reassured me—but the person behind the move: "It's that he was so nothing. He had no life, no sparkle. He never said anything interesting or funny. He was boring." *I believed the story (why would she make it up?), but I wondered why she embroidered it with so much irritation on the theme of my father's social insufficiency. Of the Provincetown years, where my parents summered in the sixties and seventies, she concluded, "He didn't do anything, he just sat there like a toad with his papers." Is this her way of taking my mother's side? But she, too, comes in for criticism, confirming my hostile adolescent view that I had come to hope was Oedipally predictable and unfair: "secretive" and (worst of all for a woman who, like the rest of the Croton group, had seriously flirted with American communism), terminally "bourgeois" (hence summer camp).*

I try to square this portrait of my father (a toad*?) with Daddy, married to my "conventional" but "lively" mother. It's true, as her friend said, that he didn't* do *anything on vacation unless my mother sent him out on a mission (to gather mussels, for instance), but was Mommy's lifelong obsession with playing tennis really so much more interesting? (After her death, my sister and I dumped the trophies and the cups without a moment's hesitation, as if we couldn't erase fast enough the traces of a passion we had refused to share.) So what if Mommy had played tennis with Sidney Poitier.*

I don't know what to do with this story. Was this why Daddy always accepted the guilty charge? Why he took Mommy's anger?

Home before dark. Our parents want us home before dark. They want us home so that we will be safe. In some ways the memoir is the revenge of a poor reader: having failed to read the signs in her life, she makes a work of art out of her reinterpretation. "For those who wished to look for them, there were clues to his sexual nature

everywhere.... Still, few people really guessed. The image he culti-
vated of a patrician, old-fashioned country gentleman must have
been very convincing. He didn't want us to know—and we didn't
want to know." It's not safe when the darkness is at home. Then
John Cheever was dying and he wanted the world to know.

A daughter outs her father. In some way, every memoir of a parent's life is an act of exposure, making the private public, telling
family secrets, violating decorum. In Cheever's case, the children see
themselves as going public in their father's place, according to his
wishes. The outing, perhaps, is not so much the fact of his sexuality,
but the revelation of the mystery installed at the heart of family love.
How can you repossess the truth of your own story when you lived
it through the ripples of a lie?

After a parent's death, the picture necessarily looks different. In
the wake of Sir Michael Redgrave's death, Lynn sorts out the
enigma of her father's behavior at home.

> Perhaps he was unwilling to take on the responsibility that comes with
> fatherhood. I don't want to imply that my father's homosexuality nec-
> essarily had anything to do with this. Interestingly, I did not know of
> his sexual orientation until I was a married adult, information carefully
> imparted to me by my husband. Although how it had escaped me till
> then I'll never fathom. Maybe I didn't want to know.
>   At any rate, knowing finally made sense of much of his behavior. It
> became possible to stop hating him for the emotional neglect of my
> mother. That was something I always knew about, because I was
> always aware that my parents maintained separate rooms and that my
> friends' parents shared a bed. ... I longed all my life to know and to
> feel that he loved me, and only in his decline and illness did he begin
> to show it. For my part, sadly, it was only as I became more the parent
> to his ever-weakening child that I could reach out fearlessly to him.
> Now I needed to forgive.

Why write about the dead? To try and forgive them for not being
better and ourselves for not knowing it. But what do we know when
we think we know?

Treetops: A Family Memoir, published seven years after *Home Before
Dark*, is about a real place in New Hampshire where generations of

Mary Cheever's side of the family gather in summer. It is also a metaphor for the stories families tell about themselves in order to feel real. This second memoir is an attempt on a daughter's part to unravel her feelings toward her mother, who is still living. It's here, at any rate, that the biographer emerges more clearly as the subject of her own story—actor and not just interpreter. Taken together, the two memoirs constitute a modern elegiac performance in which the mourner refuses to give up her dead but also rehearses more boldly her desire to take her rightful place as the family chronicler.

Treetops is divided into three parts. The final section opens with the scene of a reading from *Home Before Dark* at a New York bookstore. Mary Cheever has accepted her daughter's invitation to introduce her. She describes the sorts of things people ask her about her role as the wife and then mother of a writer. "'What's it like not to have any secrets?'" Mary answers this question by a disclaimer, saying that "she still did have secrets." What's it like to have your husband's sex life made public by your daughter? "My father was bisexual," Susan Cheever writes in *Treetops*. "My mother never acknowledged this but it turns out she knew it." What Mary Cheever's acknowledgment of her husband's sexuality meant to her emotionally will remain one of her secrets. What the daughter made of her mother's knowledge will remain one of hers. This scene comes close to revealing the living hurt banished from the mournful cadences of the memoir devoted to her father. (It's nicely perverse that she places the discussion of her relation to her mother against the public reception of the book about her father.)

The story about my father was that he was a "wolf" until he met my mother. During the four years of their engagement, she remained a virgin: she tamed him. She would never budge from that version of their life together no matter how many times I asked, incredulous. "It was different in those days," she'd say, refusing to yield to my probing. "I was always drawn to your father," she would say. "A woman can be really attracted to a man only if she's married to him." There was never anyone else. That was the story—for her, the object lesson for my sister and me.

My parents married in 1936. They married in a rented house in New Jersey, with all the Millers in attendance, and my father's mother. The opening shots of the home movie of their wedding showcase the Millers cavorting on the manicured grounds: playing leapfrog, riding bikes, being ostentatiously carefree. Suddenly, my parents emerge from the house, smiling. My mother is wearing a belted black and white, tiger stripe silk dress and a black straw hat; my father, a perfectly cut ice-cream-colored suit. (Of course, I'm just guessing, this is black and white.) My mother is twenty-two and stylish; my father twenty-nine and dapper. They match. They kiss: my mother's broad-brimmed hat frames her face. A real kiss. In full profile. I rerun the movie. I will never see that kiss again, except in the movie. Pecks and smacks, passion gone domestic.

8/12/36. "Dear Fay," my mother writes to her sister from the steamer Quebec *(my parents have taken their honeymoon in Canada).*

> *Remarkable as it may seem we had a very pleasant trip. Imagine, the two of us travelling for ten hrs. without the slightest suggestion of an argument. We had to get married to stop quarreling (knock wood).*
> *I think we're the only Jews on board. The women are about 69 and the men 74. We had a swell time last night. We danced for about an hour and then played the races. Our luck hasn't changed a bit. We're still making donations. . . The trip is very smooth and the views are incomparable. The only thing missing is the soft spoken Miller family.*
> *Mollie and Lou (Mollie Miller Kipnis).*
> *P.S. There are so many Christian Brothers on this boat that they make you ache for the sight of a mazuza.*

My mother as a twenty-two-year-old bride on her honeymoon. My father takes the pictures. My mother wears a different outfit in every shot, shows off her college French, dazzles my father—you can tell when she turns the camera on him. They married on the hope, never fulfilled, that my father would be made assistant district attorney. They married while still living at home, among the Millers.

We want, or think we want, to know what goes on between our parents: who they were before we were born, who they were when they weren't being our parents. Who are the people behind their wars, the sophisticated skirmishes of emotions and sexual disappointment in which we so often are the unwitting casualties? Would we even like our parents if we didn't think we had to?

The summer of 1981, the year before my mother died, we planned a family outing for the Fourth of July. We could have dinner in Chinatown and then watch the fireworks over the Hudson from a window in my father's office on lower Broadway. Service was despairingly slow and we were late leaving the restaurant. Forging ahead with her athletic pace and me breathless in her wake, eager not to miss the spectacle, my mother led us through the winding streets; my father lagged behind, his natural slowness aggravated by the drag of Parkinson's; my husband kept him company in a show of masculine solidarity. When we got to our viewing spot, the moment had passed, the fireworks were over, a few random bursts left to punctuate the nightscape: "You blew it, Lou," my mother jeered with an exasperated sigh. "You blew it."

Toward the end of *Treetops*, Susan Cheever discusses her parents with a novelist friend.

> "So, do you think he was a monster," I ask. . . .
> "I'm not going to say what I think, because it would be too strong," she says.
> "What's worse is that he didn't protect you, and your mother didn't protect you."
> "She had her own problems," I say.
> "Still you were her children."

The cover of *Treetops* shows the John and Mary couple at the family compound during their courtship or maybe in the early days of their marriage; a portrait of twenty-two-year-old "Mary Winternitz Cheever" in front of a tree in bloom faces the title page. "The women in my family," Susan Cheever writes, introducing the themes of her memoir, "don't tell many stories about themselves. In a family of storytellers and mythmakers they have always been characters, not creators of characters." *Treetops* is not uniquely the women's stories, however. It's about "the men who made the family famous and the women who live in their shadows." Susan Cheever places herself in the line of storytellers and creators of characters, but the myths she transmits still hover in their creators' shadows. The storytellers win out. Mary Cheever remains—whatever her personal accomplishments as poet, teacher, and writer—a daughter, a wife, and a mother. She is defined within family dramas in which men are the major players—of the family she descends from, and of the marriage she makes. As Carolyn Heilbrun argues in *Writing a Woman's Life*, "There will be narratives of women's lives only when women no longer live their lives isolated in the houses and the stories of men."

Treetops and *Home Before Dark* illuminate the different ways in which Susan Cheever, like so many literary daughters, distinguishes between her bonds to her father and mother. Despite all his obvious imperfections—his alcoholism, his philandering, his waspish moods and staggering self-involvement—John Cheever is idealized by his daughter. *Home Before Dark*, conceived, written, and published in the aftermath of the father's death, accepts his credo as an artist: The life redeemed by the art. Daughters tend to exculpate their fathers (despite their glaring insufficiency) while keeping their mothers on trial. Mary Cheever's flaws, however rationalized as the effect of her family upbringing and the stresses of her marriage, are presented with an unforgiving—or at least, unsentimental—edge. Daughters don't forgive their mothers easily, even when as women they see how their mothers' struggle with marriage plots and their own unfinished business as daughters make them alike. It's almost as though daughters can't forgive their mothers for being themselves and wanting something for themselves—beyond us. On the other hand, we don't give up on them, or on wanting something from them, which is an equally powerful form of attachment, and perhaps the fiercest. *Treetops* is a guide to the minefield of relations between two women who are also—and both—mother and daughter.

It's 1977. I'm thirty-six years old. I'm going to Provincetown for a week with my parents. This is not because I want to be with them; it's a long hot summer and I want to get out of the city. As usual I'm wretched because of a love affair that is turning out badly. Leaving town, even with them, makes me feel less pitiable—at least I'm not wretched and hot. I'm also, as usual, having a bitter, unending fight with my mother. It would be impossible to say about what. That's why it's unending. We fight because we cannot say why. How does it start? It starts because it has never stopped. This time, I screamed so loud and she remained so silent that I can't believe we will actually make this trip together. I've gone too far. But I'm wrong. Tentatively friendly, my mother calls the next morning to confirm departure plans.

I join them for their annual summer trek to the Cape; this in itself has the makings of domestic epic. Eight hours of arguments about driving, relieved by complaints about my smoking. They are going for a month. I have rented the cottage next to theirs for a week, pretending that not being under the same roof means that I won't be under their thumb. At least I'm paying my own way. The car almost has no place for me. My mother, who is driving first, cannot see out the back window. It is my job to peer through the stacks of hats and hills of tennis balls, and make out if anything is happening behind us. The trip feels eternal, especially since my mother insists on having my father share the driving. He's a terrible driver and she can't relax while he's behind the wheel. There's some point to be made here about "the man" doing the driving. "Lou," she yells, "you're drifting." I pity my father, but she's right, he's straddling two lanes.

Mary Cheever is alive and Susan Cheever might still get something from her. Beyond approval, what does the daughter want? At the bookstore reading, Mary Cheever wonders aloud whether she always knew her "daughter was capable of such an accomplishment." This kind of indirection is characteristic of the family technique. "Typically for our family," the daughter observes, "she had used a public medium to tell me something she had been reluctant to tell me in private. This was a sore point between us; a sore point that, of course, neither of us mentioned." So now, in properly postmodern fashion, we have a second public, published version of the first public revelation of private discord. Mary Cheever, Susan says, had been quoted in the press as feeling that "the book was inaccurate and that she had wished I hadn't written it." In *Treetops* we don't learn any more about what Mary Cheever felt about her daughter's family memoir. Instead, this scene becomes the occasion to define the essence of the maternal style—"remoteness is a defining characteristic of my mother's personality," the daughter explains, "developed in reaction to the stresses of her life." Remoteness is a self-protective emotional style but its effect is to leave her daughter always yearning. "Spacy absentness," she explains, is for her "mother's armor, her fortification, her unbridgeable moat." Remoteness, paradoxically, coexists with an unexpected directness, a collapsing of distance— her "disconcertingly unpredictable" social behavior. The practiced fear of being wounded, a kind of psychic numbness, seems to produce an insensitivity to the boundaries of others, and causes wounds of its own.

Do your parents love you? We try to make it come out that they do. We try, but how can you ever tell? Susan Cheever relates an anecdote in which a friend of the family tells Ben in Mary's presence how much John loved his children. "'Oh no,' she said in a surprised voice as Ben stood there helplessly. 'The only one of the children he ever *really* cared about was Fred!'" But if the effects of such "attacks of candor" are passed over without comment—after all, by that accounting, Susan is not really loved either—they no less shape the reader's view of the family's crushing approach to handling feelings. (Like Art's recasting of Vladek's maniacal stinginess as "pragmatism," Susan's version of Mary's indifferent cruelty becomes "unpredictability.")

In *Treetops* the key word Susan Cheever uses to map out the territory of domestic relations is again the term she used repeatedly in *Home Before Dark*: "confusion." As an adolescent, with or without dates, Susie can't seem to please her father; they have constant scenes, and this she concludes, forgivingly, was an expression of his "own confusion about sex." If John Cheever was confused about his sexuality, Mary Cheever was confused about "the role of class and wealth in her life." Everyone was confused about the generations. "There was always a lot of confusion in our family about who were the parents and who were the children." In a rare moment of self-revelation the daughter embraces the classic confusions of the Oedipal triangle. "My competition with my mother for my father's attention was also heartbreakingly direct." Going to parties as your father's date or his companion in your mother's place is a seduction few daughters can resist. In *Treetops* the triangle gets taken apart: "'It wasn't so much that Mummy and I were competing,' I say to my brother Ben when we talk on the telephone. . . . 'I think the problem is simpler. I love her and she doesn't love me,' I say. 'End of story.' 'But you're still hoping!' my brother Ben says. . . . My unsuccessful quest for my mother's love is the force that locks us together in our endless dance of sympathy and opposition, the dance of mothers and daughters." But the mother/daughter dance is choreographed by the father. He sets the stage for the women's pirouettes. "My father often said how much my friendship with my mother meant to him." What it also meant, she adds, was "freedom to attack her"—in life, in his journal, in his fiction. The greater confusion is this: the daughter's belief that she really *is* special. Daddy's girl. My father, myself. This is a tricky identification for a woman, especially if your father doesn't own the resemblance.

During the summers spent at Croton-on-Hudson, my mother would drag my sister and me to the tennis courts. To preempt our whining while she finished yet another set, she'd give us nickels to feed the Coke machine. Now, three decades later, while my mother plays tennis in Provincetown, I sit indoors and write letters to France where a man is thinking about leaving his wife for me. I reread the letters I've already received. He's sent me money for us to spend in New York, as proof of his intention to come. I'm thinking that he probably won't and that it would be scary if he did. Still, I want him to do this. For one thing it would cure me of a lingering passion for another married man in New York. It would be exciting. Even if it didn't turn out, at least it would be something. *After several hours I emerge and go look for my father who has been gathering mussels in the bay while the tide is out. This is what he does in Provincetown while my mother plays tennis or socializes. In the late afternoon I find him heading back to the pier carrying a pot filled with mussels. He's wearing a white crew hat, the brim pulled down over his broad forehead, but it's too late: his nose is already brick red from the sun. Despite his full pot, he doesn't look happy.*

He's not, I can tell, glad to see me. I know he'll never start, so I ask as we walk back ahead of the tide whether he's mad at me. He frowns his frog mouth and begins making the case for my mother, as he has for years. When I was in college, holed up in the maid's room that I had converted into a bedroom, my father would come in and work me over: "I can't sleep, your mother won't let me go to sleep until you apologize." "Why should I apologize when I'm right?" "You're right, but she's your mother." This is a script we both have memorized. Why can't I see that she has my best interests at heart. "She doesn't. Can't you see that?" No, he can't. He sighs. I know what he's waiting to ask me. He's waiting to ask me to apologize for the scene in New York. She feels hurt. She's making his life a misery. OK. She's wrong in this case but she means well, so why can't I go in and apologize for his sake. There's a tug—poor Daddy—that I resist. What good will it do? Will it make peace? No. Saying sorry isn't good enough. I have to mean it. Show it. Will he be on my side next time?

Walking down the beach, I see this man on the verge of frailty. He is already condemned by Parkinson's disease but it hasn't been named. No one's talking about it. The mask hasn't settled on his face, and the shuffle could just be laziness. Or age. "Lou, pick up your feet." I see this man in his early seventies, his head still handsome, edging his way slowly toward the shore. The light is beautiful. On the postcards for the Cape they call it "opalescent." At this time of day, he always says, "They should bottle it" (the light). Should I take pity on him again? Will he call me Doll again? "Doll, please, do it for my sake." No. No. He calls her Doll, too. When he's run out of arguments. Special pleading.

"You don't care if I eat shit, as long as Mommy gets what she wants, do you?" No. He actually says no.

I always thought that because I looked like my father, I was my father. He never saw it that way.

Perhaps the greatest price paid is by the daughter who wants to perform and to count for herself in a world where the parent—father or mother—has set the terms. How can you tell what's yours when the person who authored you is an author? "Few things are as confusing," Susan Cheever writes in a review of Linda Gray Sexton's memoir, *Searching for Mercy Street*, "as being the child of a famous writer. Perched on the line between life and art, the delicate division between private parents and their hungry public, a child is caught in alternating storms of privilege and deprivation." The dilemma created is not just the inevitable and exaggerated split between private and public realities, which fractures the life of any famous figure's child, but the power of the literary text to refigure your identity: finding yourself in the stuff of fiction. "My father, John Cheever," she continues, "used to claim that his life had nothing to do with his art, but even as a ten-year-old I knew better." An avid reader of her father's stories, Susan comes upon herself as a fictional little girl who gets mangled in a horrible ski accident. The importation of life (the ski trip you survived) into art is flattering. "I loved it that our lives were somehow worth writing about." But the price of finding out that you count enough to become material includes the risk of discovering that your life has been brutally truncated for the sake of a good ending. This is a double bind that cannot be resolved: "I was very proud that I was a subject for her," Linda Gray Sexton writes about her mother's poems, "but it was terrible to be written about."

The fame of a literary parent always cuts two ways. It justifies the family's self-mythologizing—the very acts of collective self-deception that Susan Cheever sets out to demystify in *Treetops*. But at the same time it provides a story so powerful that you cannot escape its effects—a story that includes you, that has a place for you, but that holds you under its spell. "Knowing her was a magical thing," Linda Gray Sexton says about her mother. "Most of the time it was fun to be with them," Susan Cheever writes, "some of the time they were magic." Writing a biography of your famous parent is one way of breaking the spell: writing back with your own version of literature and life. It can also mean keeping yourself under the spell: you write yourself back into the very story that you are trying to write yourself out of. "I had always been proud of my independence from my father," Susan Cheever declares in the preface to *Home Before Dark*. "I never intended to become his biographer." But this is a classic double bind. She depends on the very thing from which she proclaims her independence: her father—their family and his stories—are her best stuff. Linda Gray Sexton maintains, she says, "an ongoing relationship" with her dead mother, but who set the terms of that relation? In *Searching for Mercy Street* the daughter pulls out a snapshot that releases a "flood of intense, precisely detailed memories." She describes watching television while her mother lies on the bed. At one point, wanting an answer to a question, the daughter turns around and sees her mother lost in the space of her own desire. "Naked from the waist down, she is making noises and her fingers curl through her crisp black pubic hair. She pushes her long clitoris back and forth against the lips of her vagina. I drop my eyes ashamed." Having re-created this scene of trauma from her past, the daughter-biographer rewrites herself into the picture as an adult: "To write these words frightens me. What sin do I commit by remembering and speaking at last? Like some long-craved-for food finally in my mouth, words have power. Mother used to own all the words. Now I own some of them too. Once I hated her for using her voice. Now I understand why she did."

Writing about the dead is always both an end to the relation and the possibility of a new beginning. But the child of a writer rarely escapes the mesh of the parent's control of language. Owning some of the words always remains a partial mastery, biography a style of empowerment forever belated.

Susan Cheever's position as a family biographer is inhibited by another kind of double bind: a dual allegiance to the people in her family and to her ideas about writing. She can't seem to make up her mind about the ethics of her father's crafting public art out of their private experience, in part because she's been an enchanted reader of the constant transformation of her mother's life into the fiction. "Sometimes it's hard for us to separate who she really is from the dozens of literary portraits my father created," Susan writes in *Treetops*. "She was his everywoman ... and his one-woman university. ..." But a muse's life can be rough. "My father acted as if he owned her, tearing off the intimate fabric of her life and cutting it into shapes and forms to clothe the creatures of his own imagination." The artist's wife accepts her place as the cloth of experience with no rights of her own. (The mother's fabled remoteness was perhaps a fragile screen of self-protection against this dispossession.) "Being victimized," Mary admits to her daughter in a conversation about the marriage, was in her nature. Ben, who is also a novelist, argues that his father had to write the way he did; it was for his own survival. "'The trouble is,'" he is forced to admit, "'that I've ended up feeling as if I was a minor character in someone else's book.'" Susan defends her father's right to make stories out of their vulnerabilities: "'But if the stories are great, doesn't that make a difference?'" She rehearses the position, tries out its pros and cons with friends and finally with her third husband: "'A fiction writer'" he claims, "'doesn't have that kind of obligation to the few people in his family. He writes for readers.'" As a fiction writer she identifies with her father, even if as a daughter and a biographer she also feels her mother was injured in the process of making art out of life. These conversations about the ethics of John Cheever's fiction writing are, of course, meditations on the ethics of the biographer as well. What about nonfiction, she asks her husband? What definition of accuracy could be meaningful, she wonders, as Spiegelman worried about the representation of his father in *Maus*. "'It just depends,'" she concludes, giving herself the last word, "'on which facts you choose to be accurate with.'" But Fred, the father's best-loved child, who became a lawyer, remains unimpressed by the alibi of the aesthetic and condemns their father's treatment of their mother unambiguously: "'There's absolutely no excuse for what he did with Mom. . . . What he did is a major wrong. It's right up there with slavery. . . . Art is no license.'"

A memoirist also writes for readers whose judgment will be made *outside* the family, its myths and truths. It falls ultimately to us as readers to decide what seems accurate and what feels ethical. But can we know what motivates the choice or what's being concealed? At one point in *Treetops* where Susan Cheever speaks of becoming friends with her mother and describes the new intimacy between them, she also reveals to the reader two "secrets" important to her life in those years—two secrets she did not confide in her mother:

"the fact that I was in love with a married man I worked with, and the fact that my husband occasionally hauled off and hit me so hard that I saw stars and once had a black eye for a week." Secrets and betrayal, telling and not telling, the truth of the autobiographical project is always vulnerable to the selection of emotional facts, and these so-called facts themselves hostage to the unreliable convictions of memory.

We think we remember, we want to remember, and we try. What we can't help doing, though, is connecting the pieces from *then* that we have housed inside us with the feelings we have about them *now*. Representing others has everything to do with representing ourselves—over time.

Lear on the Hudson. It's a stormy weekend morning and the agency has sent a replacement. It's a man called Adonis. Like all the other home aides who have looked after my father, Adonis is black; unlike the others, he's male. My father phones to complain. He's surly, my father says, and he wants a replacement. I tell him that it's too late but that I'll come over and see what the problem is. I observe the two of them for a while. Adonis, while not sunny, is perfectly polite (unlike my father, who is shouting, out of control). Adonis is determined to do a good job, which, as he understands it, entails not letting my father out of his sight, even following him into the bathroom. At one point he tries to help my father out of his chair and my father recoils. "Don't touch me," he bellows; "I don't want him to touch me." I am transfixed by the revulsion in his voice, the panic in his face. What is he so afraid of? Gusts rattle the old windows. The rain beats against the panes. I am longing to leave, longing to go back to my books. Adonis and my father waltz around the apartment; my father shuffling as fast as he can to escape his keeper, Adonis insisting that this is what the agency expects him to do. Suddenly, I hear glass crashing. I run into the kitchen, where Adonis has followed my father to the refrigerator. The storm has blown the window out. It's raining in. My father, dressed in his shorts, starts shouting that he wants "him" out of his house. I shout back, "I don't care what you want." I don't, but there's also no way I'm going to leave him alone in the apartment with the window blown out. I call the super and have him nail wooden boards into the frame. Reluctantly, I

dismiss Adonis, reassuring him that he had been doing a good job, that he
will be paid for the entire day. The kitchen grows dark, we fall silent. I reach
for the vodka and pour my father some gin. I settle in for a long afternoon.

> My father was not a shit. He was a man
> failing at life.
>
> SHARON OLDS, "Waste Sonata"

Home Before Dark is the book of a daughter in thrall to her father, to
his self-construction as a writer. She writes in the shadow of his
death, still entranced by his personal myth, imagined in fiction,
rehearsed in the journals, memorialized by a family whose coher-
ence and identity he kept alive in part by the force of his need for it:
"the roof and settle of my existence." This is the good father Susan
Cheever keeps alive protectively, along with the accomplished
American writer. She exposes the John Cheever of the journals, the
father she didn't—or didn't want—to know. The daughter models
herself on two important pieces of his character, which she remakes
as her own: her passionate belief in family and his convictions about
what it means to be a writer. The turn she makes on the legacy is to
open the closet of the family through a genre her father left
untouched: the memoir. The idea of family seduces father and
daughter. "Our need for this community," the daughter comments
more generally, "keeps us in a cage of other people's desires and
expectations; some of us spend our lives peering out through the
bars at what seems to be a larger world."

Where is Susan Cheever in this zoo of need? She seems to be asking two questions: Do you love me? Am I a good writer? The first
has to do with what she calls her mother's "remoteness" in the face
of her children's desire for reassurance: "'I hope I won't always be
this lonely,' I would sigh, when I was an adolescent. 'Have a piece of
this nice cheese!' my mother would say, or 'Oh, Susie, could you let
the dogs in?'" The matter of her loneliness does not recur.

Loneliness is the leitmotif of John Cheever's journals and the
memoir devoted to him. Susan Cheever marks off her loneliness as a
piece of passing adolescent misery, and her writing exudes a kind of

surrounded ess. She seems more at home than homeless, at least in the space of her biographical writing. What's fleetingly palpable, though, is the way in which, as her brother Ben puts it, she's "still hoping." Longing for the love, or recognition, or reassurance she sought from her mother. Hoping and writing. The two seem to go together: "We learned from watching my father that to survive as a writer you have to just keep writing, even when editors turn you down, even when there's no money, even when reviewers savage you." You have to keep living and write past your insecurity and the cage of your unmet desires.

I check my father's diary and mine to verify details of the episode with Adonis. My father has two penciled entries, one a Monday, one a Thursday: "Window blows out." Two illegible words, then "bed." On Thursday, "Kitchen window blows out," followed by a garbled line that seems to be about the super and the repair. My diary is not much more precise, and equally succinct. Again, a November date, the storm scene appears sandwiched between worries about leaving my old job and starting a new one. "Feel so sad about leaving Barnard. At the same time I had to produce a change. How stuck it all is. But also nostalgia about my scene. What will it be like to have a new one? LK's window blows out. . . . I wish he had blown out with it. Worked all day Sunday and made a serious dent in YFS. It needs one more session. A couple of hours left on biblio for SCT. Graded grad papers. Now budget."

"How sharper than a serpent's tooth it is / To have a thankless child!" My father loved to quote that line; it was central to his repertoire. Shakespeare, for my father, was fathers: Lear, Polonius ("To thine own self be true" was a favorite injunction), Shylock. He loved the hackneyed, whatever the source, collected aphorisms, and filed them for his briefs. We groaned when he trotted out, "This too shall pass." When, Daddy, when? (Little wonder that I chose as my dissertation advisor a man who specialized in the analysis of clichés, fixed patterns of speech.)

Were we thankless?

If Mary Cheever found *Home Before Dark* "inaccurate," if she wished it hadn't been written, one can only imagine how pained she might feel about a conversation in *Treetops* in which to Susan's question, "'What did I do wrong?'" Ben's answer is "'You were born, you were a child, you made impossible demands on her the way children do.'" A mother who, her daughter says, "lived for us," nonetheless found motherhood hard because she felt unmothered. "'I was the child,'" she explains to her daughter, "'my mother didn't want.'" This legacy of not being wanted is a bond she shares with John: His parents "had not wanted another child before he was born. His conception was a drunken accident between two people who no longer cared about each other." What can ever come to erase the effects of unwantedness?

The autobiographical section of Lynn Redgrave's *This Is Living* begins with the discovery that her birth does not appear in her father's diary and ends after a visit to *his* father's grave in Australia (where Lynn had gone to make a series of Weight Watchers commercials) with a rewriting of the entry to include her new existence:

> There it was, Dad's journal for 1943, the year of my birth.
> I turned to my day, March 8th, but now it was a short entry and one of my own making. A small liberty would be allowed, perhaps. No.
> My dad would have approved, wholeheartedly. I know it now. "Today my daughter Lynn was born. I love her."

He loves me. This is one way children have of making the story turn out their way, especially when parents have had control of its shaping forces through their public prestige and their power in the family. When they, famous or not, are gone, we can finally make them love us the way we wanted to be loved when they were alive. By reinventing the inventor, you re-create the one, as Roth puts it, who created you. You repair the old wounds and inflict some of your own—that's the storyteller's prerogative. (*One of the Family*, Wendy Fairey's memoir about her mother, well-known Hollywood columnist Sheilah Graham, and the discovery—after her death—of her true father, British philosopher A. J. Ayer, ends with the question of revising family history. Fairey discusses Graham's legacy—her books and her secrets—with her daughter, Emily. "'You'll get back at her,'" Fairey's daughter ventures. "'You'll write about it.'")

Writing *Home Before Dark* and *Treetops* as family biographies allowed Susan Cheever to put her parents in their place by making them into her material. She evokes, for instance, the violence at the dinner table and her father's account in his journal both of her description of the scene as a "shark tank" and his own evaluation that Mary is the shark, not he. "Thinking of Susan," he writes, "she makes the error of daring not to have been invented by me, of laughing at the wrong time and speaking lines I have not written. Does this prove that I am incapable of love or can only love myself? Scotch for breakfast and I do not like these mornings." Does your father love you? Does he think you're any good? Does he even know you're alive? Rewriting his story is a way of answering these questions for yourself.

By the time Susan Cheever drafts *Home Before Dark*, she has become a mother. The tone of the memoir and placing of the writer's voice are bound up with that change of identity. "As I had grown more pregnant, my father had become sicker. He lost a little every day, and that loss seemed to cast a shadow over all of us. The birth of the baby didn't take away that loss, but it changed everything for me." Susan Cheever is writing not only as a daughter but as a parent, herself. The second memoir is located specifically under the sign of motherhood. This awareness of the children to come as readers reins in the emotional violence of the family biographer. There are things you cannot tell your children about their parents or their grandparents, unless you want to model a hatred you might come in turn to inherit.

Ten years after the publication of *Home Before Dark*, in *A Woman's Life* (a book described as the biography of an "ordinary woman" of her generation who tries to juggle marriage, children, and a job), Susan Cheever explains what this child meant to her in relation to her father's death. She named her daughter Sarah after her father's grandmother: "I wanted her to have a connection with this past that I was losing I wanted to mourn the loss and keep the family and family names alive. I wanted to remind myself that generations come and go and that the death of a father happens to each one." The assumption that "generations come and go" shapes this daughter's imagination in both memoirs.

The fact that Susan Cheever can conjure the names of the generations—her father's grandmother—is a mark of the ways in which a family's idea of itself also belongs to history. As part of her self-presentation in the biography *A Woman's Life*, she invokes the Cheever lineage: "I lectured Sarah," she writes of a trip to Salem she's made with her daughter to visit the subject of her biography, "on how her own distinguished Cheever relatives had once walked these docks and shipped out to China." She explains the origin of Granny's Canton china. If we all are called upon to reconstruct ourselves after the death of a parent, what is displayed here is the way in which we make sense of ourselves in relation to a particular piece of the family story. The "distinguished Cheever relatives." The legacy for Susan Cheever is that of a name that she makes her own in her signature, that she continues in the naming of her daughter, and that attaches to possessions and places. There is not always that much to own or to hand down. Sender Roth's shaving mug. Families without a tree. History without heirlooms. Genealogies broken by cataclysms. Cultures where names are *not* passed on. How do we imagine the end of the line as another beginning without the flesh of continuity or its fictions?

Your parents' child, but also an adult who is now a parent—this double position has a great deal to do with the voices that shape Susan Cheever's, Lynn Redgrave's, and Linda Gray Sexton's family biographies. Grown-up Susie and Lynny, the writer and the actress, as well as Linda, the writer, give birth to children whose parenting they seem passionately to embrace as a form of emancipation from the place assigned them in their childhoods. (*This Is Living* features a photograph of Lynn gazing longingly into her father's eyes as she introduces him to her one-year-old daughter three years before his death.) In the face of death, the fact of these children both prolongs and revises the family plot. *Home Before Dark* and *Treetops* are forms of grieving that display the fixing of loss in language and in story, but also through the music of nostalgia. In the last scene of *Home Before Dark*, Mary Cheever picks up her daughter's daughter and croons a ballad she used to sing to Susan: "Bonnie Charlie's gone away. . . . Will he ne'er come back again?" Like the stage directions for the last scene of a modern American family drama, "no one says anything as my mother twirls and sings in the corner of the room and night falls." The curtain comes down on domestic elegy.

Our sense of an autobiographical self, a self with a story, is conventionally understood in terms of generation. It's how you pass on the story that you think expresses you. This act of transmission is neither a good nor a bad thing in itself. But it is a conception of identity that has a tremendous impact on our culture's idea of self-definition. If we pause just for a moment and think about a parent's death in relation to a child who does not go on in turn to become a parent, we see to what extent our ideas about identity are interwoven with the notion that the self is bound up in plots of family time. Colette conceived her only child, also a daughter, at the same age as Susan Cheever, within weeks of her beloved mother's death. (Believing in literary models, I tried, too). The coincidence—but is it ever that simple?—of conceiving and giving birth in the shadow of a parent's illness underlines and literalizes the power of generational metaphors. To carry life in the face of death puts death in its place.

What happens when you step outside that story?

The daughter keeps her mother alive—the last image of *Home Before Dark* is of Mary Cheever, a grandmother, sitting peacefully at the end of her life in the place *her* grandfather built, "watching as darkness falls softly over the view her mother fell in love with so many years ago." And there she leaves her mother "with the rest of them, the living and the dead." But we know that this image is also troubled: her mother is not only there in a place of past time, but here in living relation to her in the present. She has both been found and left her daughter wanting.

And yet, despite the harshness of certain judgment, the old resentments are always countered by a kind of reconstituting forgiveness that comes from both the distance produced by time and the difference of view produced by assuming the parenting position. It may well be that resentment and forgiveness intermixed will forever be the legacy of memory. "In the end," Linda Gray Sexton writes of Anne Sexton's passions, "her love both damaged and nurtured." Bound in the chain of family history, unfinished business haunts us all. This is especially clear in *Treetops*.

> We children all wished in vain, as my parents had wished in vain when *they* were children, for the kind of ideal parents we saw on television and read about in comic books—parents who were unstintingly supportive and protective, parents who took care of you. There were moments when my father as least *acted* like the father played by Russell Crouse on the show he sometimes wrote for called *Life with Father*. My mother never even pretended. Still, in their own imperfect way, they did as well as anyone can do at being a parent. They did their best.

It is this belief that Susan Cheever passionately joins, even while showing the cost of such an endeavor. These two books memorialize lives lived in family as though family were all that mattered, as though it were the larger world and not just a perspective on it. "I think that family is the most interesting thing in the world," Susan Cheever comments in the course of an interview about *A Woman's Life*. "If I had my druthers, it's all I'd write about." In an odd way, what she chronicles is the intractable longing for the world of *Life with Father*, a fantasy that sustains a father's idea of himself at the expense of whatever reality counters it, a fantasy spawned in the America of the fifties. Is this a father worth keeping alive? Thinking about Linda Sexton's desire to cleave to her mother by writing about her, Susan Cheever counters: "Like Linda, I wrote about my father, but my book, started while he was dying, was a eulogy—a way of keeping our conversation going after he was buried. I couldn't write a book about him now. I know too much; I don't care enough." Why write about the dead? To remind yourself of what you can no longer bear to know.

If *Home Before Dark* was written for herself, *Treetops* was written for Susan Cheever's children: "In the years since then, as I have raised my own children and started to tell them about their family's past, I began to see that I had told only half the story—my father's story." *Home Before Dark* is dedicated to her brothers and to her daughter, Sarah. *Treetops* is dedicated to her "wonderful daughter Sarah." The last words thank her two children, her son as well as her daughter, with this closing line: "They are what I live for." (She wrote of Mary Cheever: "Her children depend on her and complain about her. She lived for us.") This shared legacy of motherhoods continues the genealogical mapping on which *Treetops* opens. The new generations of children are also connected to the literary inheritance of John Cheever. The diaries were read, written about, and published in the years following his death. The children's own families proceed in that wake as well: "In fact, the family house was so comforting and so much fun that it took us children a while to start our own families. . . . Then, in the year my father died, we all got married—Ben and I for the second time, Fred for the first. In the years since my father's illness we've had four children between us."

It's not easy to leave home, it seems, when you're part of so many good stories.

My father, in the early days of his career as a lawyer.
New York, late 1930s.

6

UNBILLABLE HOURS

> . . . I would have traded
> places with anyone raised on love,
> but how would anyone raised on love
> bear this death?
>
> SHARON OLDS, "Wonder"

"You made me love you, I didn't wanna do it, I didn't wanna do it,"
was one of the lines from songs that my father loved to belt out in
a tuneless baritone at the threshold of our bedroom—to torture us.
(He claimed that we were distantly related to the great Russian
basso Alexander Kipnis. These performances were meant to prove
it.) "Stop, Daddy, stop," we would shriek, clapping our hands over
our ears.

Can I make him love me now? Can *he* make *me* love him?

In the apartment my father lived in for fifty years I found seven date
books: from 1982, the year of my mother's death, to 1988, the year
before his own. *Dailyaide: The Silent Secretary, Daily Planner, Daily
Minder.* For a long time I couldn't figure out why my father needed
the diaries. Like radios and reading glasses, calendars could be
found in every room of the apartment. But with the approach of
each new year he asked my sister to buy him another book. The
diaries seemed at first to be a continuation of his logs: as a lawyer,
you record whatever you do for clients, what you can legitimately
charge them for—the time it takes to pick up the phone, open the
mail. You account for every move. These are billable hours. For the

last seven years of his life, after my mother's death and his forced retirement from a flagging one-man practice, the date books bore the traces of a lawyer's habits, the remains of a professional life in which your time mattered. And every entry in the diary—the exterminator, the cleaning woman, the refrigerator repairman, your daughters—keeps alive the fiction that your life is worth something because it is a life in which things happen even if you stay at home. People come *here*. People call. Reliving those years now in memory, I want to get answers to the questions that cloud my days: not just what did the end of *his* life mean to him, but what was my place in it? Did I matter?

I open my father's date book for 1988 to find tucked inside the flyleaf a copy of the deed to his cemetery plot issued by the Manhattan Fraternal Association, and scribbled across the title page, the phone number of the exterminator. There are fifty-five entries for this last full year of his life. He died the following June at eighty-two, of complications, as they say in obituaries, from Parkinson's disease. We buried him on Father's Day.

One of the effects of Parkinson's disease is the deterioration of handwriting called micrographia that mirrors the destruction of the mind. This shrunken script, that tends to run off the line and trail off like an unfinished thought, borders on the illegible. My father's once confident and florid strokes tremble and hesitate about the proper direction. He writes the way he now walks. It's called festination. You rush with tiny steps until you stall, immobilized on your feet, or fall.

It pains me to stare at the letters crunched together, drifting upwards and downwards off the lines; squiggles punctuate the page at random; lines collapse into each other. I take out a magnifying glass to decipher the tiniest words. Some entries remain illegible, the rest I transcribe onto my computer, and erase the proof of my father's incapacity—like Colette covering her father's blank pages with her prose. What's worse? To struggle with the stained detail of the page or to ponder the printed abstraction of a life drastically reduced to these isolated bits? If I don't go back to the pages, I forget how ragged the fabric of this life is. If I stay glued to the pages, I become immobilized. Like him, I go back and forth over the same narrow strips of territory.

In my diary for 1988 I find the seeds of this chapter. "For LK. I will collect his diary entries. Micrographia." Writing now from the diaries, his and mine, and remembering through everything that happened afterwards, the hospital, I've no idea what I meant. Whatever I meant, I'm not happy with what I find. A phone call I made in January 1988 to a social worker specializing in these situations: "Go to fate, timing. Use up $ since money will go *anyway*." My aunt said my father worried that nothing would be left for "the girls." Like Lear's bad daughters, we worried too: he's using up *our* money! LK became more and more frugal, buying day-old bread from the local bakery. It was day-old the next day anyway, so why not save the money?

I pore over his entries, looking for answers. I'm a literary critic and my father's life lies before me as a text. The author is dead, we know—I've explained this to my students—and you can't know the author's intentions. It's up to me to tease meaning out of fragments, to come up with an interpretation. If I transform Daddy into a paper father, and his life into a collection of signs, I can make my way through the pages more easily. The years of my father's illness, recorded in miniature strokes, become more bearable as a story—a story so familiar that even I, who played a role in it, recognize the clichés. I've become part of a middle-class soap opera. But that's not all. When I go back over these entries, it's not just a matter of professional compulsion. I'm doing something else. I'm keeping myself alive as a child. I'm still asking myself the questions I can't answer, and especially one that haunts me: Was I a good-enough daughter? I tell myself that maybe he wasn't good enough either. And this is what I've done for my entire life—figure out the score. When my parents were alive, they determined the score; now it's my turn to figure it out, dole out the guilt. I read these pages of my father's diary as though my life depended on it. However it turns out, one thing is sure. There's no new place for me in the family plot unless I invent it.

FEBRUARY

15

MONDAY

President's Day

JANUARY 1988	FEBRUARY 1988	MARCH 1988
S M T W T F S	S M T W T F S	S M T W T F S
1 2	1 2 3 4 5 6	1 2 3 4 5
3 4 5 6 7 8 9	7 8 9 10 11 12 13	6 7 8 9 10 11 12
10 11 12 13 14 15 16	14 15 16 17 18 19 20	13 14 15 16 17 18 19
17 18 19 20 21 22 23	21 22 23 24 25 26 27	20 21 22 23 24 25 26
24 25 26 27 28 29 30	28 29	27 28 29 30 31
31		

Words without thoughts never to heaven go—Shakespeare

8:00	
8:30	Ron correspondent
9:00	to meet Jay
9:30	all
10:00	
10:30	LK
11:00	LK
11:30	
12:00	
12:30	
1:00	
1:30	
2:00	
2:30	
3:00	
3:30	
4:00	
4:30	
5:00	
5:30	
6:00	
6:30	
7:00	
7:30	

JANUARY 1988	FEBRUARY 1988	MARCH 1988
S M T W T F S	S M T W T F S	S M T W T F S
1 2	1 2 3 4 5 6	1 2 3 4 5
3 4 5 6 7 8 9	7 8 9 10 11 12 13	6 7 8 9 10 11 12
10 11 12 13 14 15 16	14 15 16 17 18 19 20	13 14 15 16 17 18 19
17 18 19 20 21 22 23	21 22 23 24 25 26 27	20 21 22 23 24 25 26
24 25 26 27 28 29 30	28 29	27 28 29 30 31
31		

The cautious seldom err—Confucious

FEBRUARY

16

TUESDAY

47 « » 319

8:00

8:30

9:00

9:30   *Ron comes to visit LK and*

10:00   *to meet Jun*

10:30   *he*

11:00   *LKJ continue*
no solution

11:30

12:00   *LK*

12:30

1:00   *It appears that*

1:30

2:00

2:30

3:00

3:30

4:00

4:30

5:00

5:30

6:00

6:30

7:00

7:30

That sounds good, but what am I really doing? I reproduce the pages of his decline, make public what he meant to be private. (My parents hated that we told family secrets.) I'm no better than the family biographers whose motives I challenge in this book. They make themselves look good (or bad, which can be another way of looking good) by exposing their parents. Maybe I'm saving my skin by flaying theirs.

To whom did he write? Dear Diary always stands in for those by whom we want to be recognized, even if they're only ourselves.

My father, LK, writes to his wife, MMK, who died on April 7, 1982.

Sunday, June 27, 1982

Dearest Doll:
    While flying back home yesterday it occurred to me to record my feelings and thoughts.
    Some social history.

Dearest Doll. These pages are collected in a loose-leaf notebook with a title page headed "Random Jottings—Mostly Post-Mortem MMK." Although there is a date book for 1982, these supplementary, hand-numbered pages are more completely filled in with detail and the occasional observation or appreciation. It's as though LK creates a competent self for MMK to see. "Daddy would just be content to sit there and look at me," my mother would complain, "never do anything on his own." I think she liked having a spectator to her life, and now she's the spectator to his. LK takes care of business: *transfer of the balance from Mom's account to LK as Exec.* Tries to do exercises using a tape recorder. Works at competence: *Continued trying to clear away unresolved items, bills etc.* Goes for a checkup and reports: *Blood pressure 130/70, weight 138 lbs. Attempted to make "barley, bean and mushroom" soup. None of the cookbooks had recipes for it. So I tried to analogize the available "beef" cooking instructions.* Details the process by which he arrives at a reasonable facsimile of the soup he wanted: *It was not bad. Also I had enough to put away (freeze) two portions.* He works at it: *Nancy came for dinner and tasted my beef and barley soup and pronounced it good. She made the salad and dessert and tasted my various cheeses—she was not enthusiastic about them. Ron called during dinner and spoke to Nancy and me.* Dearest Doll. I'm taking care of myself, the girls phone and visit. Dearest Doll, look, I'm trying, look, I'm writing it down. . . .

Of the fifty-five entries in 1988, twelve are related to his illness, primarily to the issue of caretaking: Will he or won't he accept having someone live in the apartment to look after him? He wants to continue to live alone, can't see what the fuss is about. "Daddy, would you rather lie on the floor for hours than have someone in the apartment? You could catch pneumonia." Yes, he knows. It takes a very long time for me to circumvent what a therapist once called his "won't power." For a while he would threaten to kill himself implausibly (like my mother with the electric toothbrush) by drinking gin. Suddenly he just wants life to go on exactly as it is, styled by his ruses for having things his way. The log mimes the progressive disorganization of body and mind until the entry system itself collapses into silence: as the year winds down, none in October, none in November, one on the last day in December.

While he was alive, I occasionally glanced at the diaries, gratified when I visited to see my name appear: *Nancy phoned.* January 9, 1988: *SNOWSTORM ENDS NANCY COMES WITH CHICKEN SOUP.* I trudged through the snow with soup, chicken soup no less. My soup rates an entry in his life. January 16 weaves the strands together: the Lawyer, the Housewife, the Good/Bad Father, the Good/Bad Daughter. I read: *call Arnie Arnie Astrachan.* On the next line, the exchange copied twice, followed by the phone number. Writing the phone number usually means a business call. Sometimes there's a number with no name. Sometimes the number is written several times, incompletely. *Nancy.* Another line. *comes.* The verb slants upwards. Another line: *Nancy comes but does not.* Two lines skipped: *Nancy asks about my opinion to have Joanna as a nursemaid*—the word nursemaid jumps upwards off the line; *for me,* next line. Space. *Con Ed man comes in to take a reading of our meter.*

I fill in what I know, plan to research what's missing. Who *is* Arnie Astrachan? Why is LK *returning* his call? *Nancy comes but does not.* I do not stay for dinner, probably. When I was working ten blocks away at Barnard, I would stop off on my way downtown to my apartment; it was like living at home and going to school at Barnard thirty years earlier, only reversed. I no longer lived at home and I was a teacher, not a student. I was in charge of his life; he no longer ruled mine. I didn't stay for dinner. I did have a drink, a double vodka (maybe a double double) on the rocks.

I wanted someone to live in the apartment. I had, I thought, come up with the perfect solution. Joanna was a graduate student at Columbia. I would reconvert the maid's room, which had been my room in college, then a "dinette" when I moved out, back into a room for her. It had a view of the George Washington Bridge, its own half bathroom, and a separate phone line. All she had to do was be there at night; make sure my father didn't spend the night on the floor.

February 16. *Ron comes to visit LK and / to meet Joanna.* Spaces. *LK continues.* Next line *LK*. Two more lines, *It appears that.* I try to finish his thought and wind up following my memory of the scenario. Joanna hasn't moved in yet. She's checking out the scene, wondering if she can handle it. Though Joanna is kind and accustomed to the grubbiness of shared student apartments, I suddenly see my home (even if I don't live there anymore) through her eyes, in the shabbiness it has permanently acquired. Despite the valiant housekeeping efforts of the various home aides, nothing remains very clean for long. The house needs a wife.

February 17. *See entry for Tuesday. Joanna comes to visit / Ron and Joanna hit it off.* Actually, he has tried out this account on February 15—trying to write "hit it off," referring to himself in the third person as LK. (I puzzled for awhile over the LK, whether it was new. LK turns up in personal papers about his financial status: LK for what belonged to him versus MMK for what belonged to my mother. LK is the worldly version of Daddy.) *Aileen comes up as usual to / put.* Aileen, a woman who lives on the ground floor and who has dedicated herself to helping the vulnerable elderly tenants in the building, has agreed to come and put LK to bed. (She already brings him the *New York Times* in the morning. He no longer reads the paper but likes to see it.) His habit is to fall on top of the bed fully clothed; if she puts him to bed—undressed and tucked in—perhaps my father will sleep through the night. At least that's the idea. Since he won't let anyone from the agency have a key, he often ends up sprawled out on the floor, immobilized for hours, until the aide finally shows up and gets Aileen or the super to let her in. I succeed in paying Aileen through a complex fiction of benevolence; the checks coincide with every holiday in the calendar. A small army of people are enlisted in supporting my father's determination to live alone, but they have their limits, which they convey discreetly but unmistakably. This is not something that concerns my father, who seems to take it—nonchalantly—as his due. We apologize for him.

Why don't I put my foot down, as my mother would say (and do!). Because I've become caught in his system. It *is* horribly expensive to have someone in the apartment day and night. If he lives for five more years (and why not, except for the Parkinson's, the doctors say "there's nothing wrong" with him), no money will be left. Who will care for him then? So we keep on, improvising, waiting for the catastrophe, the disaster that will prove that we are right—and force a solution. But that doesn't stop me from being furious at him almost all the time. Yes, I want impossible things. I want my daddy back. The good daddy who took care of things for me, the dapper man who went to an office. Even the incompetent version, the slightly ineffectual daddy who had started to lose it before my mother died—frayed and unraveling around the edges like his three-piece suits, but still recognizably Daddy.

Every night we would wait for Daddy to come home for dinner. "Where's Daddy?" My sister and I would lean out the window and crane our necks, trying to spot him ambling down the hill. Hilarity when he stopped to talk to someone and we would signal for him to hurry, screaming into the wind: "Daddy!" The race to be the one to press the buzzer of the intercom in response to the family code—dot dot da dot dot—and then the doorbell. We would run to the door and assault him with excitement. Were we glad to see Daddy or just relieved that we were going to have supper at last? But first he had to wash his hands, soiled from reading the paper. (Reading the Times, *went the family line, was a sullying experience. I still long for a man whose first gesture when he comes home is to wash his hands.) While he was gone, we would grab his briefcase and rummage through its sections for hidden loot: a Baby Ruth, a Mars bar, or Hershey with almonds. If no candy, then supplies: yellow pads and yellow number two pencils. The brief-case smelled of mystery, of the world we never fathomed, the SEC, the courts, the names of lawyers and judges (good and bad) we would never meet.*

 Later, the routine wore thin. "The train was crawling." That was the refrain with which my father tried to ward off my mother's exasperation at his late arrival: "The liver is overcooked," my mother would announce with an edge of bitter triumph. "That's the way I like it," he'd reply gallantly. "That was your mother's idea of cooking," she'd counter, "shoe leather." (Invoking his mother generally put an end to the repartee.) Once we grew up, no one cared about answering the door, not to mention what we ate for dinner.

When I call from home and he doesn't pick up the phone, I jump into a cab. The cab races up Amsterdam Avenue—twenty-four blocks uptown, three crosstown, making every light. Too soon. Too soon. My heart pounding, I think, What if this is it, this time he's really dead. Yes, I want him to be dead when I get there. No he's alive, on the floor, looking up sheepishly, though finally unrepentant.

 May 24. Pre-dawn / left bed and "found" several people in apt. / They refused to leave and I called Police who came / The "event" turned out to be an hallucination.

 I arrived at the apartment one day and found my father unshaven, looking haggard. He recognized me but told me that he hadn't slept for several days because people dressed like the Jack of Spades were in the bedroom. I walked through the rooms with him showing him that no one was there. He seemed unconvinced. I got him to sit at the table while I called the doctor. When I came back into the room, I found him reading an imaginary newspaper, wetting his finger to turn the pages. Even though it turned out that this episode was caused by an excessive dosage of Artane, a drug the family doctor had given him when he complained about drooling, I have never been able to erase that image from my mind: Daddy, wearing his reading glasses, and turning imaginary pages.

August 9, 1988. *Anniversary of* LK *and* MM K. Next line, LK *&* MMK.

August 8, 1982, one of the loose pages. *Spoke to Nancy about the impact of reading "A Death of One's Own" by Gerda Lerner.*

August 9, 1982, one of the loose pages. *I remembered the day. I reflected on some of the events and things and sayings. I am beginning to concede to you the situation that life reflects compensations. . . .* Proud that he remembered their anniversary (always a big deal). Talking to Dearest Doll again, telling her that she was right (the story of their life). What was LK beginning to concede? That she was spared a long illness? A life immobilized by pain or stroke, brain-dead, as had happened to some of their friends? That she would not live to see what he was to become, see Lou, her handsome husband, shrink before her eyes? (Of MMK's need to be right, my sister said: "Mommy would rather be right than be loved." My father loved her anyway.) My father writes to the dead. Does Dearest Doll answer?

In the date books, the anniversary of the death appears only in 1986, the only entry for that day: *Yahrzeit candle by* LK.

January 16. *Con Ed man comes in to take a / reading of our meter.* The Con Ed man rates an entry. For fifty years the comings and goings of the Con Ed man had gone, I'm sure, unnoticed. Now they make it into personal history. "Our" meter. The plural jumps out at me. My father loves to say "we," figures out strategies for promoting his "me" into an "us" whenever he can; as though there were a family or even a couple to share the meter.

The phone drives the log. It also drives what remains of my father's life. He calls his sister-in-law Fay; his first cousin in Montreal, Gert; the occasional old friend from the couples' days; NY Tel, Universal Exterminator, et cetera. He gets called by Nancy, Ron, Fay. All the personal calls are to or from women. *Recd call* signals the remains of business transactions or a formal matter. So does, usually, *spoke with* or *spoke to*, though here I can't always tell who initiated the call. LK does not record calling me or my sister, though he does this frequently. He even adjusts to leaving messages on my answering machine. There is always a note of surprise bordering on triumph when he introduces the message, as though he can't quite believe he has mastered the technology: "This is Daddy!"

When LK gave up taking the subway to Wall Street and moved his office into the dining room, I worried that he would be bored and depressed. Depression is a common effect of Parkinson's. "Are you blue?" the neurologist would ask. My father looked blank. First, you have to get past the Greek accent, then the lexicon, finally: "Are you depressed?" Oh, no. Me depressed? The "girls" looked after him, his sister-in-law brought him almonds and prunes from the Lower East Side. He had the phone, his radios and TVs. What more could you want if you couldn't have MMK?

April 7, the anniversary of MMK's death, as he might have put it. Instead, the traces of the attempt to call Gert. *GERT IN MONTREAL / 1 (514) 555-1212 INFO / 1 (514) 555 1212 (Info) 489-6758 / 489-489-6758 / —1 (514) 489-6758 / (514)* Did he call? What prevented him from learning this number, which he had dialed so many times? Scraps of paper covered with phone numbers littered the apartment. Lists with several phone numbers, the same numbers on the backs of envelopes, the bottom of calendars. He had always liked making lists of numbers, by category: numbers for Provincetown, numbers for Paris. But now the repetition seemed to have a life of its own.

December 31, the last entry of 1988 and MMK's birthday (not noted). Instead, pencil rewritings of Gert's phone number. Maybe by not getting him a diary for 1989 we unwittingly hastened his decline. Maybe just writing the number of his beloved cousin would have helped.

When my father was first widowed, I suggested he go with an aide to the 92nd Street Y and try their senior citizens' activities. He returned home put off both by the "level" of the company and the undertones of matchmaking—scornful but probably scorned as well. There were classes in arts and crafts, group excursions, "social" activities designed for "seniors." For years birthday cards from the Y would arrive; they sent them out by the month.

My aunt brought him—in addition to the nuts from the Lower East Side—tongue from the kosher butcher. He paid her what he owed: *Fay visited me here. She brought me some items. $6.07. She invited LK to the Seder.* That was in 1987, the last Seder. It was a long time to sit. But the great unsaid was the spectacle he had become, particularly in relation to the table: drooping, drooling, dropping his food on the floor. Did my father miss the Seder? What would have been hard to give up was the food, and that he didn't have to miss. Saturday April 2, *Fay comes at about 2:30 P.M. / bringing Seder "goodies" / We do not go to the park / We stay upstairs / Fay and LK spend hour in gossip.* He rewrites the word *gossip* more clearly. The Seder comes to him. "Goodies."

In the seven years that followed my mother's death, my father became more and more absorbed by the kitchen. Once the guest in my mother's domain of mastery (except for *his* mother's old Jewish treats, which he cooked for himself and only he could digest: "matzoh brei," "gribenes," "mamaliga"; naturally, my mother thought they were retrograde). On his own, my father liked to boss us around about food. I'd call before coming and ask if he wanted anything. He always did. Stilton, figs, things he couldn't seem to get Shirley (his last home aide) to buy or wanted me to buy for him. It wasn't simple: it had to be imported Stilton, not domestic; figs on a string, not in a circle. The only thing that never failed him was his appetite. May 26, *RON HERE WITH HER OWN FOOD (CHINESE).* We usually brought something to eat. That way, you could do the visit and get dinner over with as well. Takeout Chinese was almost always what we ate. My father ended up with the leftovers and there was always a carton of rice drying out in a corner of the refrigerator.

One of the last meals I had with my father and mother took place in a Chinese restaurant on Broadway. I had just met my future husband and this was his first meal with them. We ordered a whole fish with the head on (only my father wanted the head). The waiter was impressed. Once everyone was served, my father started in on the head. He fell to it with an intensity that precluded conversation. We watched him demolish the fish head—bones, eyes, and all. Embarrassed by his feeding frenzy, my mother tried several times to intervene—"Lou!"—but there was no stopping Lou. My husband, a southerner, was astonished by this battle over the fish. Later, he also

remarked disapprovingly that my father "smacked." Though I had
never heard anyone use the verb all on its own without "lips," the
image was clear enough. Smacking was the punctuation, the mark of
how much my father enjoyed it, in case anyone hadn't gotten the
message. It used to be that silence meant that he was reading, now it
meant that he was eating. It was as though his mouth had replaced
his eyes.

The diaries rehearse the determination to record a normal life.
The horrors are evacuated. May 11, *Fell in foyer* [turquoise ink
smudged and illegible] *slight bleeding*. My father took a perverse kind
of pride in his wound, a bruise on his temple, a sign of his capacity
to survive. A badge of indifference. Not enough to send him to a
home. June 15, *Ron here. Worked on bedroom rug to try / to eliminate
odors*. The rug in the bedroom, near the bathroom but not near
enough, has that sweet and sour smell of dried urine. Is it worth
buying a new one? No, no, he protests, it's a waste of money. We try
a rug shampoo, the kind advertised on television that looks so easy.
Only when all attempts to save the rug fail am I authorized to buy a
new one, a synthetic guaranteed not to absorb odors. It's hideous, of
course, but what standards am I trying to maintain here? We already
have a hospital bed!

Parkinson's insidiously destroys certain sets of brain cells that in
turn produce physical symptoms in the body and the disruption of
the mind, sometimes to the point of dementia. Drugs like Sinemet
(L-dopa plus carbidopa), which my father took faithfully for years,
can forestall dementia but they are effective for only a certain length
of time. After that, the sole barrier between you and the loss of your
mind is your gray matter. Symptoms—drooling, for instance—can
be controlled by drugs like Artane, but in some people they also
cause hallucinations.

In the spring of 1989, my father was hospitalized for several
weeks. I reread the notes in my diary for Saturday, May 29, but this
is not a scene I am likely to forget. I came into his room and he
greeted me with a smile as he used to when he was well." "Hiya,
love." This greeting jarred with my father's more formal ways of
speaking, as though English were not his native language (which,

in a way, growing up in the Yiddishkeit of the Lower East Side, it wasn't). His speech at home was punctuated—for humorous effect —by mannerisms from the courtroom: "Proceed, madam." That day he looked up, met my eyes, and said: "I just want to take this opportunity to say I love you." This unexpected declaration—the phrasing was pure LK—magically dissolved the resentment I had walked in with, resentment built up through weeks and months of caring for someone who was no longer there. That day, a person had returned behind his eyes. I could love him again. He said he hoped this illness wasn't interfering too much with my work. I said no and meant it. "You know," he added, worrying about my sister's future as a potter, "Ronna thinks that artists don't think about money, but that's all they do think about." He repeated his wish not to be "a burden" on my sister and me. I left feeling eager for the softness of sacrifice.

The next time I saw him, he started rambling about flying stoves, and then he was gone. We never spoke again.

With my goddaughter, Annabel,
Nice, summer 1968.

Epilogue:
POSTMORTEM

Now that both my parents are dead, whose daughter am I?

Their war lives on in me. I sometimes think they are me, I am them. But which one of them? I'm still trying to sort this out. Twenty years ago, exhilarated at having gotten a Ph.D. (I had grown up believing Ph.Ds were for men, M.As, for women), I abandoned my ex-husband's name. I took the side of the Millers, aligning myself belatedly with the survivors and their stories—"Grandpa would have been proud," my mother said. Self-renaming was in the air, but rather than take a leap of fancy, I landed safely within the family. It's also true that I was not sorry to get rid of two routinely mangled names in one blow: Kipnis, followed by Clougher, and actually for a brief period, the infelicitously hyphenated Kipnis-Clougher, complete with French pronunciation. There was something appealing about the anonymity of having a name that anyone could have and everyone could spell. It meant passing on paper. But I didn't really go all the way. I kept Kipnis as my middle name, the trace of which remains as an initial in my signature. (Did my father mind the demotion of his name? Only my paternalistic dissertation advisor worried about hurt feelings. My father did the legal paper work for me and, as usual, said nothing.) When the *K.* is dropped, as it often is by people who don't know my obsession, a sense of fraudulence creeps in. I miss the letter of foreignness that reminds me of my early years as one of the "Kipnis girls." ("Which one are you," neighbors would ask in the elevator, when we visited—separately— as adults, "the younger one or the older one?" My sister's the beautiful one; I'm the one who went to Paris.) I even miss the message of quiet failure embedded in our (not the famous Kipnis) strand of family history. The double helix of identity, the legacy of two genetic stories that some live as harmony, others as complication, is a nexus of possibility that I experience as a double bind. I'm the Lou who blew it and the Mollie who called him on it. Schlemiel and survivor.

Once, when my sister and I were fighting over the best way for my father to go on living after my mother's death (the building was going co-op; I wanted him to buy the rent-controlled apartment he had been living in for fifty years, Ronna didn't), she turned on me and said bitterly: "You're just like Mommy, you'd kill to get what you want." I never thought I was anything like my mother—I identified against her, with my father (named after him, Nancy *Louise*)— but now, in my fifties, I see how I have become her. It's not so easy to know who you are like, and sometimes this changes over time. Going through my mother's clothes after her death, I found in every pocket (and she had many, many coats): crumpled-up kleenex and a wrapped coffee candy. I was struck by the regularity with which these items of personal comfort turned up. Recently, taking my (many) coats to the cleaners, I emptied out the pockets: in each I found crumpled-up kleenex (the same leaky nose) and a box of Ricola mints (the same need to have something in our mouth). My mother lives in my pockets and also in my face. Now in the mirror, I see her face. I silently measure with her the spreading pores, the advancing crepe, lines that crease even earlobes. I think: In fifteen years I, too, could be dead. That doesn't tell me what I need to know. I need to know how to live with our face, in the face of death. Beyond our face, what does this mean? It means living without that other against whom I thought I knew who I was. NKM is MMK— except for the me of my students and my books. NKM is MMK—only minus LK. Ms. Oedipus, will you never give up the ghost?

For my forty-first birthday, the first birthday after getting tenure and the last birthday for which my mother was alive, I decided to give myself a party. Still reeling from the assault of the chemotherapy treatments and for the first time in her life without an appetite, my mother insisted on preparing food. A *gougère* (a kind of French popover), her special (brandy alexander) variation on a charlotte russe (my favorite), a watermelon carved out (scalloped edges, of course) and refilled with fruit, and a grenadine dip—the centerpiece of her entertainment mode. Two students went to my parents' apartment to pick up the food—in my place. Writing now, I'm forced to admit that it would never have occurred to me to invite my mother to my birthday party, even if she hadn't been so sick.

As I was finishing this book, I read its first chapter, "Family Plots," at a feminist conference organized around the themes of the body, memory, and life-writing. I was feeling apprehensive about going public with this material, even though I knew I could expect a sympathetic audience. Still, I fretted. The night before my paper, I had a dream—the second or maybe the third dream I've ever had about my mother. In the dream I've lost my backpack, left it in a taxi going home late one night from my parents' house. I am panicked and quietly getting hysterical. Everything I have of value—most of it sentimental—is in it. Then the phone rings and a man says he has found my bag. I should come and meet him at Ninety-sixth Street and West End Avenue if I want my things back. I'm afraid to go alone, but can't find anyone to go with me. Next, I'm walking uptown on West End Avenue toward the busy intersection at Ninety-sixth Street. (This is where I went to elementary school, and where I now go to the gym.) As I approach the intersection, which is not only busy but dangerous, I see my mother coming down the hill from the opposite direction. She's walking briskly. Even at a distance, I can see that she's smiling. And I'm glad to see her, too.

When I woke up, I was amazed to have had this dream, so amazed that I recounted it to the audience after reading my paper. It suddenly seemed as though I had reached closure—only the dénouement was not my doing, it came from someone else. In "The Shadow of the other (subject)," Jessica Benjamin describes a state in which, as she puts it, the self "can and will allow all its voices to speak, including the voice of the other within." Imagining that my mother is coming to help me recover what I have lost, and owning that I am glad to see her, is no easy matter. (As my former therapist said when I checked in recently, "You're doing pretty well, considering your unconscious.") Can I really admit that there was something about my mother I didn't want to lose?

I tell myself that when I finish this book, I'll stop searching. I'll give up and move on. This will be hard, since so many mysteries remain—enigmas that bind me to the past. In *A Woman's Story*, Annie Ernaux describes wanting to close the door of inquiry—no more information. "A few weeks ago," she writes, "one of my aunts told me that when my mother and father started going out together, they would arrange to meet in the lavatories at the rope factory. Now that my mother is dead, I wouldn't want to learn anything about her that I hadn't known when she was alive." But it's difficult to resist the lure of finding out who our parents were, especially before we knew them.

After my father's death, I found several embroidered velvet pouches containing prayer shawls and other religious accoutrements among his belongings. Whose were they? Why had my father (Mr. Socialist when young, then Mr. Reform Judaism) saved them? I had never seen him and couldn't now imagine him in either tallis or tefillin, and yet there they were, stashed away in a dresser drawer for safekeeping. What to do with them? I thought about leaving the pouches one by one at the door of the many tiny synagogues in my neighborhood, where men, carrying identical equipment, go to pray in the early morning. I kept eyeing the men on my morning jogs but couldn't bring myself to ask for advice. Instead, I packed everything into a small suitcase and stowed it on the top shelf of my hall closet. To whom were they destined? I know only that the contents of the suitcase were never meant for a daughter.

Sifting through my father's papers, looking for a key to his story (who *was* that masked man?), I come upon an invitation to the unveiling of Raphael H. Kipnis's tombstone. 1935. Mount Hebron Cemetery, in Flushing. This is my father's father. The instructions indicate that you take the subway and then a trolley. I'm excited to have found this document. I'm charmed by the detail of the trolley (and wonder when the trolley service was terminated). It feels like just the thing now that I'm finishing the book: invitation to an unveiling; a title, even. But here's what's getting my attention. My father's father is buried in the same cemetery that my own parents are buried in. My father has *never* mentioned this. Not at the time of the unveiling of my mother's tombstone. Not once. How can this be? I call the cemetery. The graves of Raphael H. Kipnis and Sadie Kipnis are only three rows away from my parents' graves in the block owned by the Manhattan Fraternal Association. Almost hidden behind the weeds, the words MOTHER and FATHER are inscribed in oversized capital letters under each name (no adjective).

My father's mother suffered from diabetes. A famously good Jewish son, my father traveled the subway from Wall Street to the Bronx for almost twenty years after his father's death to give his mother her daily shot of insulin. (My mother chafed at what she took to be excessive filial devotion.) The day his mother died, my father was beside himself for not being at her bedside; he struck out against me in wild rage for keeping the phone line busy while the hospital was calling to say that his mother had slipped into a coma. I go to the cemetery and stand in front of my grandparents' grave for a long time. I cannot fathom my father's motives but what I know is clear: No child of mine will come to stand in front of my grave. I don't want to be buried here. I decide, then and there, to sell my plot.

Works Cited

Auster, Paul. *The Invention of Solitude*. London and Boston: Faber and Faber, 1982.

Bair, Deirdre. *Simone de Beauvoir: A Biography*. New York: Summit Books, 1990.

Barthes, Roland *Camera Lucida: Reflections on Photography*. Trans. Richard Howard. New York: Hill and Wang, 1981.

———. *The Pleasure of the Text*. Trans. Richard Miller. New York: Hill and Wang, 1975.

Beauvoir, Simone de. *Force of Circumstance*. Trans. Richard Howard. New York and London: Penguin Books Ltd., 1968.

———. *The Second Sex*. Trans. H. M. Parshley. New York: Vintage, 1974.

———. *A Very Easy Death*. Trans. Patrick O'Brian. New York: Pantheon, 1985.

Benjamin, Jessica. *The Bonds of Love: Psychoanalysis, Feminism, and the Problem of Domination*. New York: Pantheon, 1988.

———. "The Omnipotent Mother: A Psychoanalytic Study of Fantasy and Reality." "Father and Daughter, Identification with Difference: A Contribution to Gender Heterodoxy." *Like Subjects, Love Objects: Essays on Recognition and Sexual Difference*. New Haven and London: Yale University Press, 1995.

———. "The Shadow of the (other) subject: Intersubjectivity and feminist theory." *Constellations* 1, no. 2 (1994).

Boynton, Robert S. "The Non-Celebrity Tell-All." *New York Magazine*, August 6, 1944. Review of Susan Cheever's *A Woman's Life*.

Brownstein, Rachel M. *Becoming a Heroine: Reading about Women in Novels.* New York: Viking, 1982.

Butler, Judith. "Sex and Gender in Simone de Beauvoir's *Second Sex.*" *Yale French Studies* 72 (1986).

Cheever, John. Interview, "A Duet of Cheevers," with Susan Cheever Cowley, *Newsweek*, March 14, 1977.

———. *The Journals of John Cheever*, ed. Robert Gottlieb. New York: Ballantine Books, 1993.

Cheever, Susan. *Home Before Dark.* New York: Houghton Mifflin, 1984.

———. "Look Back in Hunger." Review of Linda Gray Sexton, *Looking for Mercy Street. Mirabella*, September 1994.

———. *Treetops: A Family Memoir.* New York: Bantam, 1991.

———. *A Woman's Life: The Story of an Ordinary American and Her Extraordinary Generation.* New York: Morrow, 1994.

Chodorow, Nancy. *The Reproduction of Mothering: Psychoanalysis and the Sociology of Gender.* Berkeley: University of California Press, 1978.

Colette, Sidonie Gabrielle. "The Captain." *My Mother's House and Sido.* Trans. Enid McLeod. New York: Farrar, Straus, Giroux, 1978.

Denby, David. "Queen Lear." *New Yorker*, October 3, 1994.

Eakin, Paul John. "Relational Selves, Relational Lives: The Story of the Story." In *True Relations: Essays on Autobiography and the Postmodern*, ed. Thomas Couser and Joseph Fichtelberg. Forthcoming.

Edelman, Hope. *Motherless Daughters: The Legacy of Loss.* New York: Addison Wesley, 1994.

Ernaux, Annie. *Journal du dehors.* Paris: Gallimard, 1993.

———. *La Place.* Paris: Gallimard, 1983; rpt. London: Routledge, 1990, ed. P. M. Wetherill. Includes radio interviews.

———. *A Man's Place.* Trans. Tanya Leslie. New York: Four Walls Eight Windows, 1992.

———. *A Woman's Story.* Trans. Tanya Leslie. New York: Four Walls Eight Windows, 1991.

Fairey, Wendy. *One of the Family.* New York: W. W. Norton, 1992.

Frame, Janet. *An Autobiography.* New York: George Braziller, 1991.

Frazier, Ian. *Family.* New York: Farrar, Straus, Giroux, 1994.

Gates, Henry Louis, Jr. *Colored People: A Memoir.* New York: Knopf, 1994.

Goleman, Daniel. "Holocaust Survivors Had Skills to Prosper." *New York Times*, October 6, 1992.

Gordon, Mary. "My Mother Is Speaking from the Desert." *New York Times Magazine*, March 19, 1995.

Gornick, Vivian. *Fierce Attachments.* New York: Farrar, Straus, Giroux, 1987.

Hayes, Daniel. "Autobiography's Secret." Ms.

Heilbrun, Carolyn G. *Writing a Woman's Life.* New York: W. W. Norton, 1988.

Herodotus. *The Histories.* Trans. Aubrey de Sélincourt. Harmondsworth: Penguin Books Ltd., 1973.

Heron, Liz, ed. *Truth, Dare or Promise: Girls growing up in the 50s.* London: Virago, 1985; rpt. 1992.

Hirsch, Marianne. "Family Pictures: *Maus*, Mourning, and Post-Memory." *Discourse* 15, no. 2 (1992–93).

Irigaray, Luce. "And the One Doesn't Stir without the Other." Trans. Hélène Wenzel. *Signs* 7, no. 1 (1981).

Johnson, Barbara. "My Monster/My Self." *A World of Difference*. Baltimore and London: Johns Hopkins University Press, 1987.

Kaplan, Alice Yaeger. "Theweleit and Spiegelman: of Men and Mice." In *Remaking History*, ed. Barbara Kruger and Phil Mariani. Seattle: Bay Press, 1989.

Kingston, Maxine Hong. *The Woman Warrior: Memoirs of a Girlhood among Ghosts*. New York: Random House, 1977.

Kofman, Sarah. *Rue Ordener, Rue Labat*. Paris: Galilée, 1994.

Laub, Dori, and Shoshana Felman. *Testimony: Crisis of Witnessing in Literature, Psychoanalysis, and History*. New York: Routledge, 1992.

Lejeune, Philippe. *On Autobiography*, ed. Paul John Eakin. Trans. Katherine Leary. Minneapolis: University of Minnesota Press, 1989.

Lorde, Audre. *Zami: A New Spelling of My Name. A Biomythography*. Trumansburg: Crossing Press, 1982.

Marks, Elaine. "Transgressing the (In)cont(in)ent Boundaries: The Body in Decline." *Simone de Beauvoir: Witness to a Century. Yale French Studies*, 72 (1986).

Mead, Margaret. *Blackberry Winter: My Earlier Years*. New York: Simon and Schuster, 1972.

Morrison, Blake. *And when did you last see your father?* London: Granta and Penguin Books Ltd., 1993.

Oakley, Ann. *Taking it Like a Woman*. London: Jonathan Cape, 1984.

———. Interview in *Beauvoir's Daughters*, BBC, 1992.

Owen, Ursula, ed. *Fathers: Reflections by Daughters*, with an introduction by Ursula Owen. London: Virago, 1983.

Oxenberg, Jan, writer and director. *Thank You and Good Night*. Red Wagon Films, 1992.

Phillips, Adam. *On Flirtation: Psychoanalytic Essays on the Uncommitted Life*. Cambridge: Harvard University Press, 1994.

Presser, Jacques. In *Uit het werk van dr. J. Presser*, ed. M. C. Brands. Amsterdam: Athenaeum Polak & van Gennep, 1979.

Ramazani, Jahan. *Poetry of Mourning: The Modern Elegy from Hardy to Heaneus*. Chicago: Chicago University Press, 1994.

Redgrave, Lynn. *This Is Living: How I Found Health and Happiness*. New York: Dutton, 1991.

Rich, Adrienne. *Of Woman Born: Motherhood as Experience and Institution*. New York: W. W. Norton, 1976.

———. "Split at the Root." *Blood, Bread and Poetry: Selected Prose, 1979–1985*. New York: W. W. Norton, 1987.

Roth, Philip. *The Facts: A Novelist's Autobiography*. New York: Farrar, Straus, Giroux, 1988.

———. *Patrimony: A True Story*. New York: Simon and Schuster, 1991.

Rousseau, Jean-Jacques. *The Confessions*. Trans. J. M. Cohen. London: Penguin Books Ltd., 1953.

Sexton, Anne. "Housewife." *The Complete Poems*. Boston: Houghton Mifflin, 1982.

Sexton, Linda Gray. *Searching for Mercy Street: My Journey Back to My Mother, Anne Sexton*. Boston and New York: Little, Brown, 1994.

Shulman, Alix Kates. *Memoirs of An Ex-Prom Queen*. New York: Knopf, 1972; rpt. Academy Chicago Publishers, 1985.

Spiegelman, Art. Interview, "A Conversation with Art Spiegelman," with John Hockenberry. *Talk of the Nation*. National Public Radio, February 20, 1992.

———. *Maus: A Survivor's Tale: My Father Bleeds History*. New York: Pantheon, 1986.

———. *Maus: A Survivor's Tale II: And Here My Troubles Began*. New York: Pantheon, 1991.

———. *Projects: Art Spiegelman*. Exhibit at the Museum of Modern Art, December 17, 1992–January 28, 1992.

———. "Saying Goodbye to *Maus*." *Tikkun* (September–October 1992).

———. Letter to *New York Times*, December 22, 1991.

———. Public appearance with Jules Feiffer. Unterberg Poetry Center, 92nd Street YM–YWHA, November 23, 1992.

Steedman, Carolyn Kay. "Landscape for a Good Woman." In *Truth, Dare or Promise: Girls growing up in the 50s*, ed. Liz Heron. London: Virago, 1985, 1992.

———. *Landscape for a Good Woman: A Story of Two Lives*. New Brunswick: Rutgers University Press, 1987.

———. *Past Tenses: Essays on writing, autobiography and history*. London: Rivers Oram Press, 1992.

Stephens, Mitchell. "Jacques Derrida." *New York Times Magazine*, January 23, 1994.

Suleiman, Susan Rubin. *Risking Who One Is: Encounters with Contemporary Art and Literature*. Cambridge: Harvard University Press, 1994.

Warner, Michael. Introduction. "Fear of a Queer Planet." *Social Text* 29 (9,4) 1991.

Woodward, Kathleen. *Jipping Street* (1928), rpt. London: Virago, 1983.

Woodward, Kathleen M. "Simone de Beauvoir: Aging and Its Discontents." In *The Private Self. Theory and Practice of Women's Autobiographical Writings*, ed. Shari Benstock. Chapel Hill and London: University of North Carolina Press, 1988.

Woolf, Virginia. *Moments of Being*, ed. Jeanne Schulkind. New York and London: Harvest/HBJ; second edition, 1985.

———. *A Room of One's Own* (1929), rpt. New York: Harcourt, Brace, and World, 1967.